GAZE

The Man. The Player. The Coach.

**LINDSAY GAZE &
GRANTLEY BERNARD**

Published by:
Wilkinson Publishing Pty Ltd
ACN 006 042 173
Level 4, 2 Collins St Melbourne, Victoria, Australia 3000
Ph: +61 3 9654 5446
www.wilkinsonpublishing.com.au

Planned date of publication: 12-2020
Title: Gaze: The Man. The Player. The Coach.
ISBN(s): 9781925927504: Printed — Paperback

A catalogue record for this book is available from the National Library of Australia

A catalogue record for this book is available from the National Library of Australia

Printed and bound in Australia by Griffin Press, part of Ovato.

CONTENTS

Foreword 6

Introduction: Operation Successful, Patient Died. 9

PART 1 - THE MAN **15**

A Mother and Three Brothers...............................16

The Howling Dog...27

Having a Kick...34

Surgery and War...43

My Most Important People...................................49

Flipping and Renovating.......................................55

Backyard Business 61

A Cottage by the Lake 66

PART 2 - THE PLAYER **79**

The Real Godfather 80

The Fighting Gazes..86

No Roman Holiday...92

Tokyo to Mexico...97

A Dot in History...108

Whistleblowers...115

PART 3 - THE COACH 121

The Georgetown Play..................................... 122

Olympic Terror. 136

Eddie and the Mexicans. 148

Seven-point Spread...................................... 159

Not Bad for a Rookie..................................... 177

Say a Little Prayer....................................... 185

Politics and Pros. 200

Winning Time.. 213

Linda and Maggot.. 226

No More Timeouts....................................... 242

POSTSCRIPT 249

LAST WORD 255

ODE TO MARGARET

Some say heaven is up there, somewhere above the blue.
But I say heaven is here on earth, sharing my time with you.
Heaven is right here and now, just look around our home.
It's a walk in the park, a kiss in the dark, holding hands
when we're alone.
No gospels Matthew, Luke or John, they're not the words for me.
The only words I need, show my faith in thee.
And when it comes that final time, let me be the first to go.
For you are much the stronger, this I'm sure you know.
And if there is another place, I'll prepare it and you'll see.
We'll share it there together for all eternity.

Lindsay Gaze

FOREWORD

Lindsay Gaze is a national treasure of the rolled gold variety.

Whether it was sweeping the back courts of the Albert Park Stadium – his home in every sense for many years – striding up and down the sidelines of a state league game for his beloved Melbourne Tigers or walking the international stage with the Australian Boomers, Lindsay was the man for any task or challenge.

He never sought fame or fortune and was equally comfortable talking to the parents of a potential Melbourne Tiger as he was rubbing shoulders with the movers and shapers of world basketball.

His coaching style was simple and uncomplicated, and beneath that sometimes-furrowed brow, creased facial lines and early onset of grey hair, lay a brilliant mind.

My earliest memories of Lindsay came in the late 1980s as basketball was taking off in Australia.

Back then the sport was becoming more appealing to an inquisitive media. Like many sports reporters, I'd been raised on a diet of football, more football and more football with some cricket thrown in during the warmer months.

But the National Basketball League was beginning to take off, the NBA boom – propelled by Michael Jordan – was exploding and kids were taking up the sport.

The Herald, then Melbourne's major afternoon newspaper, asked me to take on the basketball 'beat', which was something of an honour for an aspiring young reporter.

My old sports editor Ron Reed gave me some sage advice. 'Get to know Lindsay Gaze,' he said. 'He'll give you his time and will help you.'

That was code for 'you know nothing about the sport' – which was right – but Ron's words resonated and I made sure Lindsay's details were at the top of my contact book (no mobile phones back then).

Lindsay could not have been more accommodating, and I became a sponge for knowledge. I listened to his every word, observed how he dealt with all manner of people from seat 1A at the courtside media table.

Of course, Lindsay wasn't just a coach. He was a tireless administrator and somehow balanced working in the sport from 9am-5pm (those hours might be a tad conservative) with coaching at nights and weekends. He was a true all-rounder.

I had the good fortune to tour the United States a couple of times with Melbourne Tigers and was blown away by Lindsay's standing on the college basketball scene. He was international royalty in the eyes of many college coaches and administrators.

On one of those tours, Lindsay invited a prospective US import to suit up with the Tigers. A big, hulking figure met Lindsay in the reception area of our hotel and I just happened to be in Lindsay's company at the time.

I offered to leave and allow Lindsay and the import to talk business, mainly of the on-court variety. 'No, stay,' he said. 'You might learn something.'

The import and Lindsay sat down at a small table and Lindsay immediately went into coach mode. He grabbed salt and pepper shakers, a small sugar bowl and some cutlery and proceeded to give the import an insight into the famed Melbourne Tigers' Shuffle offence, moving his coaching 'props' around the table.

The import nodded occasionally as he took it all in. After 10 minutes or so, he shook hands with Lindsay and said he was looking forward to meeting his new teammates.

That was Dave Simmons' introduction to basketball – the Australian and Lindsay Gaze way – and what a profound impact that had on the game both here and now on the NBA scene given Simmons' son Ben is an international superstar.

Some might say Lindsay's greatest contribution to the game was his son Andrew, but that is selling him, and Andrew, way short. His family and, by extension, his basketball family, shared equal doses of love, admiration and respect.

After reading his memoirs, I'm sure you will agree with those sentiments.

Michael Lovett

INTRODUCTION: OPERATION SUCCESSFUL, PATIENT DIED

Operation successful, patient died. It is a saying used and passed around the Melbourne Tigers for decades. While it sounds contradictory, it offers a lesson in sport and in life. Quite simply, while you might do the best you possibly can, and do exactly as you are supposed to – by law, by conscience, by instruction, by instinct – things do not always turn out right.

In the basketball sense, we might say it when we run a play perfectly, exactly as diagrammed, only for the shot to roll around the basket and fall out rather than in. There is nothing else to do except go onto the next play knowing you did your best.

That was why, after losing a game to the West Sydney Razorbacks by one point, I still walked off the court with something close to a smile on my face. It had been one hell of a game and it was the way basketball is supposed to be played. Don't get me wrong. I was not happy about losing. But the overriding factor was the game and the sport. It had been just a brilliant exhibition of basketball and should have provided pleasure for whoever saw it, regardless of what side of the result you were on. I guess that has always been my overarching view: what is good for basketball is good for everyone involved in it.

Conversely, the same could not be said about the night the Tigers played Illawarrra Hawks in Wollongong during the 1991 National Basketball League (NBL) season. The score at the finish was 186-158. The Tigers won, but it was an embarrassment to basketball. The Hawks' game plan was to simply shoot the ball as quickly as possible every time they had it, and try to press on defence. That meant we slipped into the flow of the game, taking the opportunities presented. It was lunacy. It was a blight on the game. It was not the right way to do things.

In life, it is about doing what is right, even if the consequences might be grave. Perhaps even more than doing what is right, it is about doing the right thing. There is a difference.

In some ways, it is a reminder there are always people less fortunate, people not blessed with the same opportunities, people always looking for their first break in life. When I consider my personal version of operation successful, patient died, I have come off the operation table – in life and basketball – many more times alive than deceased. For that, I have a lot to be grateful for.

Life served up a few lemons as a young child, but the love and guidance of my mother, and the mateship and support of my two brothers was unrelenting and constant. They gave me life lessons and the push into basketball that changed my life and made my life what it is. That is a priceless gift.

Similarly, Ken Watson was perhaps the most singular influence on my life, especially when it came to basketball. One of Australian basketball's greatest and most genuine servants, Ken was my surrogate father and the man who mapped out my basketball career on and off the floor, when neither of us had a map – or real plan – to follow. Without Ken and his counsel, I would not have the wife and family I do now. I would not have had the privileges of world travel and Olympic Games representation.

Without Ken, I would not have had my coaching career or the life experiences that came with being, initially, the caretaker of the Albert Park Stadium and then general manager of the Victorian Basketball Association (later named Basketball Victoria), a role that had more tentacles than an octopus.

In some ways, the games and competitions at Albert Park looked after themselves. It was the add-ons that kept life interesting, like the young girl who collapsed while training one Saturday morning. Neither a doctor, nor a paramedic, I did what I could as the only person on the spot and she came good. Fortunately, she was wearing a bracelet identifying her as a diabetic, so there was some indication of the problem. Or it was having to placate *Candles* Wells after he showed up angry one Wednesday night brandishing a hammer while games were being played. I was able to calm him and ushered him out. It was only later I wondered if my actions were brave, smart or foolish. I went for the third option.

It was the more poignant events that shaped your feeling for the job and the place. It was being a counsellor to a young staff member with an unplanned pregnancy. It was dealing with the tragedy of a player – a big, strong, strapping young man – collapsing and dying on the court during a midweek domestic game. It was coming to terms with a contractor falling through a skylight while working on the stadium, never again going home to his family, and the family never again seeing their husband, father, son and brother.

Basketball has presented me with some of the most amazing opportunities a man could ever wish for. Some of the opportunities did not come without some sacrifice and hard work. But it is fair to say a lot of the rewards outweighed the sacrifice and the hard work, even if they did come with the occasional brush with, or reminder of, one's mortality. Like when I was driving on black ice during a tour of the United States. The car went sideways and, somehow, continued on the road in the right direction, but with me facing the wrong way by 90 degrees. Had a car, bus or truck come the other way, I would have been ashes. Or it was surviving a hairy approach and landing at an airport in West Virginia. On disembarking, we learned a plane carrying the Marshall University football team and its supporters had crashed on approach to the same airport in 1970, killing all 75 on board.

The good has overshadowed the bad by a long way, and a lot of that good has been because of the people who shared the journey with me, and the people I met, befriended or stumbled across.

Among them was Bruce Johnstone, the godfather of St Kilda Saints during the 1960s and '70s, bankrolling the club through his illegal gambling activities, or what he referred to as the 'grey zone'. Known as *Bruce the Bookie* and usually one step ahead of the police, Bruce was a great friend and great company and there wasn't much Bruce could not get done via his underworld connections. Even when he went to Brazil for a tournament with the Saints, Bruce managed to catch up with Ronald Biggs, the most notorious and on-the-run member of England's Great Train Robbers.

There was Jim McGregor, an American coach who made his living in Europe by putting on tours, promoting games and securing sponsors, a percentage of all three going to him. If Jim had some cash in his pocket, a drink in his hand and a woman on his arm, he was content, even better if the woman was a rich widow. In fact, Jim once had surgery for testicular cancer. As he came out of the anaesthetic, Jim's first question to the nurse on duty was whether he would still be able to function in the bedroom.

There was Moose Leonard, a US college player we faced on one of our overseas tours. I never met Moose, but I did see a post-game interview with him. When asked about his team and its performance, it seemed Moose was about to enlighten the viewers. 'We got tree plays,' Moose told the interviewer. 'We got "One" … and … I forget the other two.' For the rest of that tour 'tree plays' became a popular catchphrase among our players.

There was the player we had on the Tigers who had more grandmothers than most of us. He was an import and I will with-hold his identity to protect the guilty. In tears, he came to me and said he had to go home to the US because his grandmother had died. I was immediately sympathetic and understanding, and he went home to pay his respects to his grandmother. Not too long later, he came to me again, looking upset. His grandmother had died, and he needed to go home. Again, we had no problem. But when a third grandmother died not long after …

Perhaps one of the greatest mysteries and pleasures I had over the years was the amount of mail I would unexpectedly receive from people I had never met. There was a young girl who wrote to me asking for help with a school assignment. I replied, she replied, and we corresponded for several years until we finally met after a Tigers game one night. There was a letter from a man in Belize asking me to clarify one of basketball's rules. How or why he chose me to ask, I have no idea. There was a letter from a man in Papua New Guinea. Every sentence started and finished with 'anyway'. He wanted to know how to purchase some uniforms for his team. We sent him a set and he was most grateful. It was a reminder of the time PNG played at the Australian Championship. The team played the first game barefooted. We were able to get some shoes for them for the second game, but there was no improvement in performance.

In a sense, this book is a letter. A letter to the people, the basketball community – locally, nationally, globally – my friends and loved ones. It is recognition and thanks for the contributions they have made to basketball and to my life.

Operation successful, patient died? I would say things have worked our pretty well.

PART 1

The
Man

A MOTHER AND
THREE BROTHERS

The screams coming from my parents' bedroom woke my brothers and me. The screams of my mother were not new as she suffered constant abuse from my father. But this time, the screams triggered a vow we had taken years earlier. We had declared to each other that, when we were strong enough to do so, we would defend our mother against our father. On that fateful night, our pact held. The ensuing action was brief, but conclusive. My oldest brother, Barry, suffered a broken tooth, while Tony and I endured no more than psychological damage. But we had honoured our pact and our mother, and hopefully disgraced our father for his vile actions.

It might be true that opposites attract because my mother was a magnificent woman with many positive qualities, while my father might be generously described as a vagabond of life. My mother was a hard worker, conscientious, diligent and loyal. My father was the opposite: full of ideas and trying to make a fast buck without actually having to work for it. My mother was a constant guiding light and shining star for me, Barry and Tony. My father really only provided a lesson in not what to be.

Born in country South Australia, my mother, whose name was Avis Mitchell, became known to everyone as Pat. Incredibly, the school she attended had just 12 students and two of them were named Avis. So she became Pat, which evolved from her father always calling her 'Pet'. My mother would ride her pony to school every day, eight kilometres there and eight kilometres back. She was one of six children and they all loved sport and all were successful in their own rights.

One sibling was an international speedway rider and excellent engineer; one won an Australian amateur golf championship and invented pipe-bending equipment that became a standard tool for plumbers; one was a horticulturalist, managing the turf and gardens at Yarra Bend golf course and Flemington racecourse; and one was a well-regarded committee member of a major greyhound racing club. Of my mother's siblings, her brother Clem, had a profound influence on me. He quoted great philosophers and shaped my views on religion, politics and governance, even though I was too young to realise it at the time.

On the contrary, my father – whose name was Albert – was the only child of British migrants and led a protected life, almost tied to his mother's apron strings. In fact, his mother prevented him from joining the Boy Scouts and nor was he allowed to play sport because both ventures were deemed too rough. The family was quite comfortable financially and my father managed to save enough money to buy a share in a racehorse that won Adelaide's Grand National Steeplechase. The family also owned three houses in inner-suburban Adelaide and my grandmother declared they would be a legacy for her three grandsons. My brothers and I never believed that would be the case and we were eventually proven right.

My parents were married in Adelaide during the Depression in the 1930s and all three Gaze boys were born in the South Australian capital, me the last in 1936. We shifted to Melbourne when I was about four and my father had moved into entertainment, hoping to make his name and money. Neither panned out. He was a chorus singer for JC Williamson, which owned and operated theatres and presented stage productions throughout Australia. When it was apparent he would not make it as a singer, my father moved into stage management, which was more his go.

Unfortunately, that role also involved my father trying to get his sons involved in the theatre and being on stage. He wanted us to develop a routine to help fill space between acts, but we were reluctant to say the least. Under his orders, I did take the stage, carrying what was supposed to be a glass of water on a tray. I would do balancing tricks and swirl around, all while keeping the glass perfectly still on the tray. Then as I walked off stage, I would let my arm drop to show the glass was actually glued to the tray. It might have got a few laughs from the audience, but I thought it was a fairly pathetic routine and I never enjoyed it.

Of more enjoyment was some backstage work, usually during the school holidays. By now, my father was stage manager at the Tivoli Theatre, which was Melbourne's most popular vaudeville venue. One job was to operate the spotlight. With no training and only the knowledge of where to flick the switch to off for a blackout, my instructions were to just aim the equipment at the performer. There was also the task of moving props between acts. While this was labour-intensive for brief moments, it also provided some up-close moments with the performers, some of whom were internationally renowned. But nothing could top the Follies Bergere and its cast of glamorous showgirls. The laws of the day allowed the showgirls to be naked on stage, as long as they did not move. But when they did move around backstage, it was a spectacular education for a pre-pubescent lad.

The theatre did not provide a reliable income stream and my father tried several jobs in between producing Casson's Gaieties at community halls in Footscray and Prahran. He was a travelling salesman, pushing bed linen; he was on the road with a circus; a bottle stacker at a glass manufacturer; and a bus driver, quitting because he was annoyed with the company directive that drivers had to wave to each other when passing in opposite directions.

There were also small business ventures: a newsagency, a delicatessen and light delivery service – all mainly managed by my mother. My father bought a panel van to operate the delivery business and he never got rid of it. People offered to buy it, but he always refused, believing it would be a valuable asset one day. When he was dying, Tony and I went to visit him for the first time since we were children. Unable and unwilling to forgive my father, Barry did not. Instead, he went to my father's house, where the panel van was sitting up on blocks. Barry took a sledgehammer and destroyed the car.

Throughout her marriage, my mother was the backbone and strength of the family, enduring my father's increased drinking, drunkenness and acts of violence against her. But on that fateful night when my brothers and I took matters into our hands against our father, it basically freed my mother. The next morning, she packed and took her three boys away from a terrible life. During and after her marriage, my mother worked hard and had several jobs, including being an usher at the theatre. When she was in hospital during her final days many years later, I asked her what part of her life she enjoyed most. She told me it was when she worked in the theatre because her workmates were her friends. It was so ironic the theatre provided such pleasure for my mother after it had been a frustrating vehicle and ambition for my father.

There is no question my mother had a hard life, but she also had a full life. She was dedicated to her family. Her hard work, attitude, love and guidance were why Barry, Tony and I became successful in each of the fields we pursued. She had set the example and we followed, each in our own way, and each determined to do her proud.

By the time I was 13, the only skills passed down to me by my father were how to handle a spotlight and how to not be like him. But Tony had been taught how to repair cars and became adept at restoring old vehicles, and Barry had been educated in a system for gambling. The bookmakers welcomed my father, his system and his money, and they probably hoped for the same with Barry. The system was designed to start with a significant bank of money, spread the bets and win small, accumulating the winnings. It took discipline and Barry did it well enough to basically pay his own way through college as he studied to become a qualified wool classer. But, eventually, Barry was too much of a gambler and preferred to bet using calculated information, a hunch or a good guess.

As the oldest brother, Barry had an influence on Tony and me, and he got me involved in gambling by laying his bets while he worked. One of Barry's mates was the son of a bookmaker who fielded at the races, trots and greyhounds, and Barry got a job with him as a *penciller*, keeping track of the bets. It was almost like giving Dracula a job at the blood bank. As Barry worked, he got me to place his bets after scouting for the best odds. I became good at getting good prices and Barry became poor by losing his bets.

One time, doing Barry's legwork even cost me a decent amount of money. I was circling the betting ring at Olympic Park dogs, trying to find the best odds for Barry's bets, when I felt a hand reaching into my pocket. Instinctively, I grabbed the bloke trying to pickpocket me and made the most boisterous disturbance the betting ring had ever witnessed. I was only a teenager, but I was mad as hell and, with my hand around this bloke's throat, dragged him to the police room on site.

As I shoved him towards a couple of police officers and started to explain the situation, they almost greeted him like a long-lost friend. They made him strip and made a couple of jokes about the off-white colour of his underwear, and then told me they needed to keep the money he had grabbed in my pocket as evidence. It was 10 pounds and quite a sum of money in those days. A while later I asked a police officer I was familiar with what had happened to the case. He said they let him go because he grassed on another criminal. But I never got the 10 pounds back, and it was my 10 pounds. I was doing the betting for Barry and I was the one losing money.

The thrill of the punt led Barry to become a greyhound trainer, owner and breeder, and he was quite successful in his own right. But he was always looking for a lurk, a way to beat the bookies and make a killing. Inevitably, the best laid plans would go awry and either the bookies got the cash or Barry missed the chance to make his money.

My mother used to talk about books she had read. One of them was *A Stone for Danny Fisher*. A boxer who fell on hard times, Danny Fisher scrambled to make money on the black market and gradually rose to financial success, only for the underworld to end his life. So I refer to Barry as the Danny Fisher of betting and greyhounds, but without the gruesome ending.

Interestingly, Barry would marry a girl named Avis, the same name as my mother and Mum's friend from school. But before that life-changing event, Barry played a persistent role in what would become a life-shaping event for Tony and me. It took almost two years, but Barry eventually persuaded Tony and me to give basketball a try. It was one of the best things he ever did, and Tony and I continued in basketball long after Barry had made his last lay-up.

In almost every facet of his life, Tony is a self-made man with very firm ideas and opinions. You do not have discussions with Tony. You have debates, and they are debates he has to win. Tony is very sound with his judgments and dogmatic in his beliefs. So much so that if his boss made a suggestion on how to do something, Tony had no problem coarsely informing the boss he should keep those suggestions to himself. That is not to say Tony was only stubborn. He is incredibly intelligent, ambitious, driven, innovative and successful in various fields.

As was often the case in our day, Tony left school early to become an apprentice tool and die maker. Such was his skill in that field he helped create the die to manufacture artificial heart valves. In essence, Tony has played a big hand in saving people's lives. But, given his personality, intelligence and talent, there was always going to come a time when Tony would become his own boss. That was how he became a chicken farmer.

As with everything, Tony was thorough and meticulous with his planning, research and preparation, and devised some of his own methods, which were innovative to the poultry industry. The basic idea of chicken farming is to breed chicks, feed them until they reach a certain age and/or size, then kill them to sell to the big poultry distributors or direct to supermarket chains. But there was a sizeable mortality rate among chicks, so Tony devised a method of creating mist to keep the chicks cool during the summer and increase the productivity of the business. The motivation for Tony was to improve the conditions of the chicks and chickens, which then improved his business. It was logical and it was successful as Tony developed one of Australia's largest privately-owned chicken farms. Unfortunately, it did not necessarily earn him acclaim from within the industry.

The big players heavily controlled the poultry industry, right down to who supplied the chicken feed and what was in it. It actually might have been considered a cartel as the big breeders and companies tried to squeeze the competition and control the industry for their own gains. There were often meetings between the various owners and Tony would attend to represent and protect his interests. While some demurred to the big bosses around the table, Tony did not. As always, he had his point of view and did not back away from voicing it, even when it differed from the man at the head of the table. The tension was palpable and eventually he was shafted by the cartel and he sold out.

The next venture for Tony was breeding ostriches. Every part of an ostrich has some commercial value, so there is no waste, as long as the bird survives the first months of life. Just as Tony had things running smoothly and a reduced mortality rate with the young birds, the bottom fell out of the ostrich market. Then came a move into coffee, growing plants and harvesting the beans. The trial produced beans good enough to win second place at the local agricultural show, but a drought and a personal illness ended the coffee venture. Unfortunately, a try at goat farming was knee-capped by rustlers, and a deal to clear land for timber went sour when the other party shot through.

Even though Tony was incredibly clever, he was incredibly unlucky. In some ways, it was a similar situation for him as a basketball coach, helping pioneer the rise of the women's game in Australia. As coach of the Comets, Tony won nine state titles and led the Australian women's team at the 1967 world championship before turning his hand to coaching men, where success was measured in different ways. I often said Tony got the 'John West players' – the players rejected by the best teams – in line with the slogan of the canned tuna giant. Regardless, Tony took players and developed them as individuals and they improved the teams he coached. For nine years, Tony was coach of Dandenong Rangers, turning Michael Tucker and Mel Dalgleish into Olympians. Such was the mark of Tony as a man and coach, several players followed him from Dandenong to Frankston Bears, winning the South East Conference title and admission to the National Basketball League. Having orchestrated Frankston's rise, Tony was unfairly pushed out when the Bears departed the NBL after just two seasons. In fact, Tony was shafted. That pretty much ended his coaching days apart from involvement when he moved north to Ballina. Up there he discovered a kid named Nathan Crosswell and sent him down to play in the NBL with the Tigers and several other teams.

In among all those career moves and lively ambitions, the three Gaze brothers always had the support of their mother. Except for playing football. She was always worried we would get hurt. As I was the youngest, she probably worried about me more than Barry and Tony, but she would often watch us play basketball when time and work allowed. Her first priority was to make ends meet for her family and she worked incredibly hard, usually in several jobs, to ensure that. We always had her support and she was always a good judge of talent and character, so it was worth listening if she passed comment on a player after a game.

As her eyesight faded in her later years, Mum was devoted to the Royal Victorian Institute for the Blind, which became Vision Australia. Mum played indoor bowls there, and her underlying competitive spirit emerged. The team qualified for the State Championship final and travelled to Seymour for the match. But the other team failed to show. Mum called me to ask for advice: should they claim a forfeit and the win, or should they offer a replay? They arranged the match for another date and won, but Mum never claimed any personal victory because she was only a reserve.

Another time, she telephoned to ask me to speak to the Vision Australia group, to offer some motivation ahead of a big tournament. I went along and saw that indoor bowls for the blind is not the most athletic competition, but it was one of the most inspiring events I have seen, because of the people. They were vision-impaired people in their 80s, all mates, all trying to win and all having a good time.

Such was the dedication, camaraderie and feeling within the group, Mum could not miss a Friday of indoor bowls. Even when she was in hospital, she would check herself out every Friday, go to bowls and return to hospital to continue treatment, eventually passing away at age 89. That demonstrated Mum's attitude to life and to people. She was always there for anyone who needed her or her help. That was why my brothers and I were there for her as we heard those dreadful screams coming from her bedroom.

THE HOWLING DOG

Like almost every Australian teenager, I was drawn to alcohol in social settings with my peers. Fortunately, I realised rather quickly that I was a pathetic drunk. With a few beers under my belt at a dance, I could be mouthy, boisterous and sometimes typically anti-social.

Being heavily involved in Australian rules football as a teenager, beer was a common element of the social scene, whether after games or after training. One night after training with Melbourne Under-19s, it was announced we were having a pie night. Also on the menu was an 18-gallon keg of beer. Playing in the Sunday league, beer was a staple and a financial income for the sly grog shops that sponsored us.

I had been dubious about alcohol as a kid, and my experience with the demon drink was limited to social occasions. I was never a pub drinker. Usually it was with footy teammates or my peer group, which was influential in me downing a few beers.

The turning point for alcohol and me came after an end-of-season football event. We had been to a dance and, rather than dance, I drank. I drank way too much. At the end of the night, my mates put me in the car and took me home. Halfway there, I ordered them to pull over. Feeling green around the gills, I vomited into the gutter until there was nothing left to give. Later on, they told me that while I was vomiting, a dog in the distance was howling at the moon and I observed, 'There's someone just as crook as me'.

When the stories of the night in question were relayed to me, I realised how much the alcohol had impaired my judgment and my ability to function as a normal member of society. I would not say it was frightening, but it was, no pun intended, quite sobering.

From that night on, I have never been drunk again and cannot remember the last time I had what might be called a drink. There were two reasons: I never again wanted to be in a situation where I could not control my behaviour; and I realised the taste of alcohol never really appealed to me. So why continue? I didn't. I have never condemned others for drinking and I never had a no-drinking policy for any of my teams. It just wasn't for me.

In fact, I can recall a conversation with my uncle when I was just a boy. He was a student of philosophy and had many and varied views. He told me there are two opportunities for you to judge someone's personality accurately. One is when they are drinking, and the other is when they are playing sport. Over the years, I found it to be a remarkably true observation because, in those situations, your defence mechanisms are lowered and your natural instincts emerge. People get to see what your character is when your judgment is impaired by alcohol and you are under the pressure of trying to win.

In later years, I considered my dalliance with beer to be my vaccination against alcohol. Like a flu injection builds your immune system to avoid a dose of the flu, I had just enough alcohol as a teenager to prevent me from drinking as an adult.

Similarly, I had a vaccination against religion, a vaccination against smoking and a vaccination against gambling. My brother Barry had the vaccinations as well, but I joke he had an overdose when it came to the gambling injection. I would never suggest Barry was a problem gambler. He just liked the idea of having a punt and trying to beat the bank.

My father claimed to have a betting system that worked, and Barry took it on. The system actually worked, and Barry paid his way through college with the winnings. Because he was usually working or in class, Barry would often get me to place his bets. In fact, I became such a regular at the bank to take money out of his account, the teller would see me come through the door and ask, 'Two fives?'

The system was a mathematical formula that required splitting bets and being disciplined. The basis was that you needed a large bank and were prepared to win small, eventually winning big over the long haul. Barry stuck with the system, but eventually, like most gamblers, preferred to punt on instinct and judgment rather than rely on mathematical probability, and he rarely let an opportunity pass.

When Barry and I played football together, I noticed during one game that he was getting a lot of attention from one of the trainers. I was worried he must have been injured, hence the need for the trainer to be at his side. My concern about his wellbeing was misplaced. In those days, the results of the races were posted on the scoreboards at football grounds. When the result of each race was posted, Barry would get the trainer on and give him instructions about the bets to be placed on the next race. I think Barry was more concerned with the results from Flemington or Caulfield than he was about the result of the game he was playing.

With his interest in gambling, Barry developed an interest in greyhounds and actually became quite a successful owner, trainer and breeder. But being a habitual gambler, Barry could not resist the temptation of trying to make some fast cash over and above the greyhound's prize money. He was always looking for a lurk and a way to get one over the bookies. He always wanted to get the odds in his favour and then make a quick killing. It just didn't always work out that way.

There was really nothing that could be done on race days to swing the odds in your favour, but the trials were a different matter. At the trials, the strategy was to give the dog a run and experience the track while providing as much misinformation as possible. Most of the track-watchers were bookies and their off-siders, trying to scout the dogs, especially those that had not raced previously, so they could set their odds. It was cat-and-mouse with dogs, and Barry played the game.

There was a time Barry dyed one of his dogs for a trial, knowing it would impress and the buzz would have the bookies winding in the odds on race night. Sure enough, the dog romped home in the trial on the Monday and was set for the race on the Thursday. But when he tried to wash the dye out of the dog's coat, it went from black to orange. The dog had to be scratched and the jig was up before Barry had had a chance to race. The dog actually turned out to be quite good and quite successful. Just never with the right odds.

Then there was the time Barry decided to have one of his dogs run dead at a trial so he could get better odds a week or so later. The plan was the dog would walk to the track – tied to the car driven at a slow pace – so that it would be too tired to race fully. It was sound logic, but the dog recovered before the trial and bolted it in. The only problem was Barry now could not get any decent odds on race day.

Another time, Barry gave a dog a shot of whiskey. It didn't win the trial, but it was the happiest greyhound at the track. There was always good planning, even if the execution did not come up to scratch. Or perhaps luck was running the wrong way, like when Barry went to England to buy a dog from one of the sport's pre-eminent breeders.

It was a magnificent looking dog with all the credentials and pedigree to be a champion. After quarantine and some training, Barry put the dog in a trial, which was required before it could race. He found a low-key trial, hoping to keep word quiet about his impending champion. The lure started, the gates flew open, and Barry's dog went nowhere. It poked its head out of the box, looked right, looked left and sat down. The dog never raced, but its breeding provided several good dogs for Barry to race.

Unlike Barry, I would not even bet on the sun coming up. I guess Barry's outlook on gambling was that he has never given up trying to convert others. He gave me a birthday present in recent years that summed it up. The gift was a multi-bet he had laid on my behalf, taking one leg on an American National Football League game and a second leg on a National Basketball League game. If both legs won, I would get a present. If one or the other didn't, I would get nothing. I got nothing.

Aside from laying bets for Barry, my only experience of gambling came in what I considered to be a perfect, no-lose situation for me. As a teenager hanging around the Chapel Street pool hall, there was money to be made without needing to put your hand in your pocket. It was called *playing the stick*, and it came in handy for me to gather some spending or holiday money.

The attendees at the Chapel Street pool room were what might be best described as less-than-desirable. There was the odd bit of trouble, but nothing too severe. The one flashpoint I do remember was some old-fashioned debt collecting. One of the pool players owed money to another local. As he leaned over the table to play his shot, the gent who was owed the money leapt from behind and drove his face into the table. The green felt turned red and the message was received and understood.

The idea of playing the stick was I, and others, would play pool for someone who was not a good player and had more interest in betting on the outcome. If I won, I would get half the winnings. If I lost, there was nothing. It was a no-lose situation for me. Sometimes, you even played for more than one gambler at a time.

The game was Kelly Pool, where the gamblers each put a nominated amount of money into a pot, with a percentage for the house and the rest for the winner. Each player drew a number for order of play. The gamblers would even bet whether their number would be higher or lower. There was another random and secret draw for a number between one and 15 to indicate which ball was yours to pot. If another player potted your ball you could not win the pool. But there was a second-chance element that required you to pot every other ball and create a *double header*.

It was not uncommon for a game to be won by the first shot. The *marker* would separate the rack of balls by punching the cue ball into the top of the stack of fifteen balls, and the first player would take his shot from the other end of the table. Make a good first shot and get good position on the next, and that could finish the game. The quick games were good for the house because that meant more revenue from the players and more bets for the gamblers.

I must admit there was one time when curiosity – or perhaps spontaneity – got the better of my anti-gambling policy. We had made a stop in Las Vegas during a trip to the United States, and took a wander down the famous strip to take in the sights and sounds. As we were about to call it a night, I spotted a poker machine that only needed one cent to play. I put my penny in the slot and prepared for a massive windfall. The handle on the machine did not move a millimetre, again giving me another immunisation shot against gambling.

The other vaccination I might have surreptitiously had was to keep me away from meat. I don't really know why or how it came about, but I have been largely vegetarian from a young age. I might eat some seafood and chicken now and then, but red meat, sausages or stew have been off my menu for as long as I can remember.

There was no religious or moral reason for it. It just happened. It may have been that when meat was rationed, we didn't have it and I never acquired the taste for it. When we did have meat on the table at home, I just didn't relate to it. I could devour potatoes, cabbage, lettuce or tomatoes. But meat just didn't do it for me, so I just didn't eat it.

Food, in general, has never been a big thing for me. I have never been a big eater and I can easily miss meals without noticing or realising. My mother was a very good cook, and I remember once telling her that if there was a pill to replace meals, that would do me fine.

There was no pill that I know of to keep me off the drink. Not that I needed it. Not after the night of the howling dog.

HAVING A KICK

The sports master at Prahran Technical School was an enthusiastic chap with a strong interest in the school football team, which included my oldest brother Barry. Four years ahead of me at school, Barry had all the attributes of a good footballer, so it was assumed Tony and I would follow suit.

Alas, my early efforts for the school football team were not considered quite up to standard. In reporting about the latest football match, the sports master announced at a school assembly that he was 'very pleased with the school spirit shown by Keith *Mousey* Franklin and Lindsay Gaze for their work as boundary umpires'. He noted quite pointedly that neither boy had the talent, and was never likely to have the talent, to play football for the school, but they were valuable members of the team, regardless.

While *Mousey* might have been pleased with the praise for his team spirit, I was quietly offended. I believed I would and should have a chance to play school football at some stage before I left Prahran Tech. It was a belief that was stronger and larger than I was at that stage of life, still being left at home by my brothers because I could not keep pace during a kick-to-kick session or a hit of tennis.

But things change and so did my body between the ages of 11 and 14. From an uncoordinated lightweight weakling, I became captain of the school football and tennis teams, head prefect and held the important responsibility of being in charge of the sports equipment.

Living in Melbourne, it was almost impossible not to have an interest in Australian rules football. Buoyed by my growth and development, football became my sport, playing for the school during the week and a junior team on the weekends. While I was never a top-line champion, I did get close to the edge of the elite Victorian Football League (now Australian Football League) with Melbourne Under-19s.

I spent one season with the Demons and may have had a profound effect on legendary Melbourne coach Norm Smith's move to ban his players from using the dropkick, a skill now defunct.

In those days, the Under-19 teams played the curtain-raiser to the senior teams. On this particular day, we were playing Collingwood and I flew to take a spectacular mark on the half-forward flank. The roar from the gathering crowd was enough to inflate my confidence and opinion of just how skilful I was. Within goal-kicking distance, I went back to prepare for a shot at goal. Chest pumped out, I approached and drew back my foot. I then drove my foot into the wet turf, creating a divot the size of a moon crater while watching the ball dribble to the man on the mark a couple of metres away.

The drop-kick always had some risk about it. You just had to have good timing to make it work. Like the time I took a mark at the front of the goal square. With distance no problem, I went back to the top of my approach feeling confident. The man on the mark was trying to distract me, jumping around, waving his arms. It was of little use. I came in, stubbed my foot, made contact, the ball dribbled to the man on mark, then caught its end on the ground and bounced over his head for a goal. As a wise man once noted, it is better to be lucky than good.

After my season at Melbourne, my brother Barry pestered me to join him at Prahran in the Victorian Football Association, a step down from the VFL, but a very good competition. I usually played as a centre-half forward and would have a run in the ruck now and then. But my football career came to an end by the time I was 21, knowing I would have to make a decision between it and basketball. Funnily enough, Prahran kept me on its list for two years after I stopped playing. The officials would tell me to just go down for a run when I had time. But I never did.

I did have a genuine enjoyment playing football, maintaining my amateur status throughout. But it would be a lie to say I was never paid to play football.

While playing for Melbourne and Prahran, I also played for a team sponsored by Wilson's Hotel in the infamous Sunday League. The league was not affiliated or recognised by any governing body. It was notorious for plenty of illegal activity and the undesirable element it drew to watch. It was basically an underground competition played in full view of the world.

What made the Sunday League so enticing was the money available for the players and the punters. The teams were sponsored by pubs, sly grog shops and SP bookies, and all had a keen interest in the outcome of the games, especially those they were betting on. The Sunday League was a good front for illegal business. The pubs would supply a post-game barrel to generate some revenue on a day they were closed. The sly grog shops did their best business on Sundays - and during the week after 6pm - when pubs were closed. The SP bookies were always on the lookout for someone to take money from.

The games themselves were good standard, probably close to VFA level, despite a tendency for violence and overt physicality that was a feature of football in the 1950s. It was brutal and I did cop a few king-hits. My mother Pat attended one game, but she was so frightened I would be hurt that she never went again. There were good crowds, usually three or four deep around the ground, providing an atmosphere and a buzz, especially when there was some decent betting going on, which could be a good thing for the players.

If we won the game and you played well, you would likely get a sling from a winning punter. He would give you a slice of his winnings as recognition and appreciation of your efforts. Even as a dedicated amateur, I did not turn down the slings that came my way, especially when it was hard to make ends meet at home.

A sling might have been as much as 10 pounds, or 20 if a punter had a big win. That 10 pounds was a lot of money back then. Not quite a week's wages, but enough to say, 'Thank you very much'. More often the sling was five pounds, which accumulated if you looked after it. You wouldn't get a sling every week, but when you did, it was welcomed. Fortunately, I won the best and fairest award a couple of years in a row in the Sunday League, so the cash rewards were nice.

Quite often, top-level players would appear in Sunday League games as ringers, taking the field under assumed names to avoid detection from the VFL or VFA authorities. There were also players who had played in the VFL, but were standing out for a year to gain a clearance to another club, tied by the Coulter Law of the day.

Among the players of note, I recall, were Athol Webb, who went on to be a prominent small forward in VFL premiership teams for Melbourne; Bobby McKenzie, another Melbourne player with the ability to drill amazingly accurate torpedo punts; and twin brothers Gordon and Norman Yemm, the latter gaining more fame as an excellent professional sprinter and actor, featuring in many shows, including *Homicide*.

But one player I shall never forget, or ever forgive, was a bloke named Lionel Ollington. Better known to everyone as *Nappy*, he was the organiser and promoter of illegal two-up schools around Melbourne. Good enough to play a handful of VFL games with Footscray, *Nappy* was a top-class rover and a member of our Wilson's Hotel team, which was a regular in the finals.

One season we finished on top of the ladder and qualified for the second semi-final, which meant we would advance to the grand final with a win or get a second chance if we lost. I was playing in the ruck with *Nappy* as my rover. At the opening bounce, I palmed the ball straight into *Nappy's* path. He executed a brilliant blind turn and kicked the ball straight down the full-forward's throat. Except it was the opposition full-forward. *Nappy* had kicked the ball the wrong way, and I immediately twigged that *Nappy* was playing dead. He had backed the opposition to win. I yelled out to the coach to get *Nappy* off. He moved him out of the action to the forward pocket and we eventually won the game.

As a betting tragic, *Nappy* had a theory for that semi-final that he felt was win-win for everyone, especially for him. Because our team was the favourite for the semi-final, *Nappy* could get better odds on the opposition and make a killing when we lost. Then he would load up on our team in the preliminary final because our odds would have drifted after the loss. We would win, Nappy would win and off we go to the grand final. But the plan was scuppered when we won the second semi-final and the grand final two weeks later.

Many years later, I discovered that a very good friend of mine, Bruce Johnstone, was in partnership with *Nappy*. A classic rogue in the best sense of the word, Bruce was an illegal SP bookie and two-up operator. Whenever Bruce was out of town, *Nappy* would oversee the two-up operation. During those periods of Bruce's absence, the two-up business never made money. *Nappy* was always gambling the profits. When Bruce told me that *Nappy* was his business partner, my response was succinct: 'Tell the bastard I have never forgiven him'.

I have always enjoyed watching football and following Melbourne, whose premiership drought at the time of writing was 56 years, and I always enjoyed chatting to football coaches about their philosophies, tactics, advancements in sports science or whatever was topical. With my basketball background, I always felt football could do more with structured plays to advance the ball rather than exist to kick long and hope someone could take a mark. That is being simplistic, but not overly simplistic when a game plan consisted of kicking long with the wind and trying to keep control and play near the boundary when going against the wind.

While football now is played with a distinct game plan and various tactics and strategies to enhance ball movement, there was a real reluctance to consider such things during the 1970s and 1980s. I spoke to Keith McKenzie, who was coaching North Melbourne, about how a better structural set-up could help. His response was that it was easier for basketball to do so with a round ball that was predictable.

I also crossed paths from time to time with Ron Barassi. Born a few months apart, we played at Melbourne at the same time. But Ron was already in the senior team and on the way to becoming a genuine legend of the game as a player and coach. What I always admired about Ron as a coach was his desire to go beyond the norm and look for ways and means to make his players better and to win games.

With Melbourne, Ron was a pioneer of bringing Irish Gaelic footballers to Australia, a move that was a success with players such as Sean Wight and Jim Stynes, who won the Brownlow Medal, Australian football's highest individual honour. Our discussions over time included the idea of recruiting an American big man with the aim of dominating the ruck hit-outs or going forward as a marking target. I was convinced recruiting and training an American much taller than regulation Australian footballers was a winner. Ron was not so convinced. There was talk Ron had recruited a mid-sized American, who was a good athlete. But I was thinking of someone like Mason Cox, the big kid Collingwood got from the US in 2015. Imagine Cox 30 years ago. It would have revolutionised the game.

Another time, Ron asked about the methods of screening defenders and invited me to demonstrate to his players how the screens should be executed. If there was a chance to help get players open, especially to receive the ball from kick-ins after a behind, Ron wanted to know about it. I took a group of players down to one end of the ground during training and started explaining and working on the screening action. The players eventually understood and executed the concept and became enthusiastic about it. But I'm not sure if Ron ever implemented it in a game.

I often debated football with David Parkin, who coached Hawthorn, Carlton and Fitzroy and has one of the sharpest minds in any sport. He invited me to speak at a football coaching course, so I started by asking the attendees about their tactics. What did they do if they were two or three goals ahead late in the game? The answer was to stack the backline. I asked if the tactic worked. The answer was yes. So, I threw a question back at them. If it works in the last three minutes, why wouldn't it work in the first three minutes? If they could devise a method of transition from defence to attack, as we do in basketball, it would work. Most of the football people in the room struggled to get their heads around it. Modern football is now overloaded with tactics and strategies that have been borrowed and adapted from other sports.

I really did enjoy my time playing football. It was only a brief speck in time, all things considered, but it gave me great perspective on sport and life and allowed me to cross paths with all manner of people. The fact I was not invited back for a second season with Melbourne Under-19s was probably a factor that shaped my future. Had I been invited to return, football might have become my priority and the Melbourne Cricket Ground – one of the world's great stadiums - a regular feature in my life.

As it was, I was on hand for the exhibition match at the MCG during the 1956 Olympic Games. Two teams were chosen – one from the Victorian Amateur Football Association and a combined team from the VFL and VFA – and all the players had to be amateurs to fulfil the Olympic charter. My brother Barry was named in the centre for the VFL/VFA team, and I was chosen as one of three emergencies.

But by 1956 I was heading towards a choice between football and basketball. If I wanted to have a chance of getting to the top – or as close as I could – I knew I needed to focus on only one sport. It dawned on me the pinnacle of football would be to play on the MCG and I had already done that. If I could become the best I could playing basketball, I could play anywhere in world, and at the Olympic Games. It wasn't such a hard choice.

SURGERY AND
WAR

There are only two things in life you absolutely have to win: surgery and war. To lose at either likely means death. But I would happily submit to the surgeon's scalpel on a regular basis than have anything to do with war.

Thankfully, I have never had to face the horror of war, and I commend and admire all those brave souls who have. But my days of National Service duty still remain the worst time of my life. As a conscientious objector, being in the army was anathema to my core beliefs and I did not hide those beliefs during my undistinguished period in uniform.

Used during wartime to draft men into the army, navy and air force, National Service had been reintroduced to Australia in 1951. Every Australian male was required to register on their 18th birthday and be ready for a call-up. That put me right in the middle of it and in uniform.

Going into my three months of full-time duty, I already had a slanted opinion of those I would be joining at the Puckapunyal army camp. I had been told those in the army were too lazy to work and not courageous enough to steal. I think I met enough of those men during my National Service period.

The three-month period was divided into two months of so-called training and one month of 'active' service. I was designated to the ordnance corps. Basically, the ordnance corps was responsible for maintaining supply of weapons, ammunition, vehicles and other necessities to the front, and to provide mechanical repairs. In short, if we were in a war, we would be delivering the guns and bullets to the front line.

But the whole thing was just so inane, ridiculous and an incredible waste of time. Trained monkeys could have done what we were being asked to do, and they might have done it better. They might also have taken more interest than me, too, which often resulted in Private Gaze being disciplined and given extra duties such as kitchen duty or guarding the trucks overnight, just in case a foreign enemy infiltrated the camp perimeter. Adding to my frustration was knowing my brother Barry was doing his National Service in the air force and seemed to be spending more time at home than on the base at Laverton.

The conditions imposed on the trainees were poor and it seemed every day was Groundhog Day, especially when it came to meals. We would be called into formation, march to the mess hall, eat and march back. Every day was the same food, and being vegetarian, the powdered scrambled eggs became repetitive and unappetising very quickly. That explained why I lived on condensed milk for most of my time in the service.

Given I was not in the mood to be there in the first place, my rebellious streak took over and I organised a strike. Technically, it might be considered mutiny, albeit on a small scale. The sergeant called for the mess parade and nobody fell into line. Everybody stayed in their tents. It was simply our way of saying there had to be a better way, and the army responded in typical fashion. You didn't have to eat, but you still had to fall-in, march to the mess hall, go through the food line and march back.

For the life of me, I just could not understand why blokes were there if they had a chance not to be. During the first two weeks, one of the blokes in our unit had a knee problem. I told him he'd just received the golden ticket, that the injury was his way out of National Service with a medical discharge. He was reluctant at first, but eventually he was discharged and thanked me for it when I met him later.

Still, the majority of blokes wanted to be there. Camaraderie was developed, they had some fun, it was a new experience for them, and maybe they had nothing better to do. It seemed the army didn't have anything better for them to do, either.

Perhaps because my enlistment papers mentioned I had experience in painting and decorating, I was put in charge of a group ordered to paint the roof of a shed. The roof didn't need painting, but those in charge needed to find things for us to do, especially if we had been detained on the weekends as punishment for some menial misdeed. It was a nice day, so we turned on the radio to listen to the football and we made short work of the roof. I told someone to find a broom and someone else to take the paint bucket onto the roof. As he poured the paint from the bucket, I used the broom to sweep it across the roof surface. The job was done in 30 minutes, and we reported back to the Non Commissioned Officer. The only slight issue on his inspection was the paint dripping out of the downpipe.

Similarly, there was the time we were asked to dismantle a shed, expecting it would take the best part of a day given we were issued a crowbar, a hammer and a couple of sundry tools. As we pondered the job ahead, we spied a bloke working in an adjacent field with a front-end loader. I went over, explained the situation and he was only too happy to help. The shed was dismantled in 20 minutes and the NCO was again left scratching his head.

The ultimate nonsense job came when we were in camp at Bandiana, just outside Wodonga, for basic training. I had been in hospital with measles and returned to camp just in time to receive orders to report with four others to Hut 54. The job was to empty Hut 54 of all munitions and transfer them to Hut 75. The next day were told to report to Hut 75, remove the munitions and transfer them to Hut 54. That was it. 'No fucking way am I doing that,' I told the NCO. 'You can put me in the brig, you can do whatever you want, but this is a mindless activity just to keep us occupied. If you want it done, fine, but do it yourself. I'm done.' I sat on my bum for the next two weeks.

All this rebellious behaviour was done in anger. I didn't believe in war, I didn't want to be in the army, wasting three months of my life, and I certainly didn't want to partake in ridiculous exercises that made a mockery of what was supposed to be military training. I'm not religious, but God help Australia if any of us had had to go into a combat zone.

Fortunately, God was also on offer during National Service training. We were told we had a choice every Sunday: church parade or undertaking more menial tasks. I opted for church parade. I had been able to get into some debate with the padre about religion, spirits, angels and evolution, and it was good to unleash the stupid restraints of army life. But sitting at church listening to the sermons only served to frustrate me as the padre offered counter-arguments to my debating points without me having the chance of rebuttal.

By the end of my training, I had had enough and those in charge knew I had had enough, so there was no point fighting it. In fact, my mockery of National Service got to the point of the ridiculous itself when I reported to the parade ground only a couple of steps removed from the character Corporal Clinger in the TV show *M*A*S*H*. From memory I had my underpants on my head and various items of clothing mismatched and out of place. The NCO could only shake his head and try to ignore me.

Yet there was no ignoring the army, even at the end of the three-month period in camp at Puckapunyal and Bandiana. There was still a requirement to commit one night per month and two weeks per year with the Citizens Military Force, today known as the Army Reserve. Basically, we would turn up to the drill hall, do little, learn even less and be paid for it. More useless and futile military non-activity.

During the two weeks of camp, we would go somewhere in the country with the idea of learning how to pitch tents and take part in a mock battle. The tents were no problem. The mock battle was another matter. Told one day we would be going out that night, the bivouac was called off due to rain. Another night we were sent out to set-up security cordons designed to intercept the 'enemy' and told to await further instructions. We sensed the 'enemy' approaching so I tracked down the commanding officer to alert him to the situation. After being ignored for several long minutes I gave up and returned to our post. Then a whistle blew and we returned to camp. We never got to confront the 'enemy' and that was the closest we came to a mock battle.

But my army career came to a fitting end after a showdown of sorts over pay. We would line up alphabetically, approach the pay window and the paymaster would mark off your name and hand over the money. I got to the window and was told there nothing for me due to non-attendance. I blew up, made a bit of a fuss and went to leave the drill hall. The exit was guarded by a soldier with a rifle, which he lowered to prevent me leaving. Bad move. I took the rifle off him and threw it across the drill hall floor.

Not surprisingly at my next parade night, I was told to report to the Commanding Officer. I assumed I would get a dressing down for my actions with the guard and his rifle. So imagine the combination of bemusement, hilarity, astonishment and incredulity that coursed through me when the CO asked if I would be interested in a promotion and more responsibility. I bit my lip and politely declined. What system would have a recalcitrant, non-conformist in its ranks and then offer a role of responsibility? It was probably a fitting end to my army life.

My time in National Service really was the most futile, unproductive and irritating period of my life. When there are only two things in life that you absolutely have to win – surgery and war – I would happily take surgery without anaesthesia over war any day.

Victorian State team: Henry Perazzo (referee), Bruce Pizaro, Bruce Cooke, Ken Watson (coach), Peter Bold, Mintauts (Chopeye) Raiskums, Gordon Busby (referee), Percy Foster (president), Lindsay Gaze, Bill Wyatt, Geoff Heskett, Peter Bumbers, Colin Sholl, Maris polis, Bob Denholm (team manager).

Victorian State team circa 1959.

Victorian State team early 1960s.

Victorian State team early 1960s.

Victorian State team early 1960s.

Aussie team heading for the
Rome Olympics in 1960.

Lindsay at training.

Lindsay Gaze
in action on
the court.

Melbourne Tigers representing Victoria on their first tour of the
USA.

Lindsay Gaze lay up. Note referee on the court looking like he is too late to defend.

The last international game at Albert Park Basketball Stadium, May 1997: Melbourne Tigers v University of Arizona. Melbourne Tigers 118 – Arizona 114.

Melbourne Tigers, a very special group. Peter Byrne (Olympian and IT consultant), Ian Speed (IT consultant), Tony Gaze (national women's coach and successful chicken farmer), Bill Wyatt (Olympian and successful businessman), Mal Speed (chair Basketball Australia, chair NBL, CEO International Cricket Council), Frank Woodhouse (successful businessman and opera singer), Alan Mayhew (dentist), Bobby Hall (dec), Ray Watson (Olympian, Professor of Mathematics), Lindsay Gaze, Roger Boulton (distinguished Professor Emeritus Department of Chemical Engineering University of California Davis), Ian Watson (Olympian, dec).

Australian Olympic team 1972.

Australian
Olympic
Team 1972.

Ray Tomlinson and Stu Inman,
the first USA coach invited to
conduct clinics in Australia.

Lindsay and Andrew Gaze after winning the 1993 NBL championship.

Lindsay Gaze coaching.

Perry 'Rocky' Crosswhite and Ken James teaching a young Andrew Gaze some basketball moves.

Lindsay and Andrew Gaze after winning the 1997 NBL championship.

Margaret relaxing.

Wedding group: Margaret and Lindsay, Tony Gaze
and Wendy Eltis.

Margaret and Lindsay in
back yard of Albert Park
Basketball Stadium.

Margaret dressed
in red.

Lindsay decorating flowers.

MY MOST IMPORTANT PEOPLE

Anybody who has known me for a long time knows I am not a social animal. In fact, some might accuse me of being anti-social and I will have no argument with them. In my younger days when my mates and I would attend a dance, they would be chatting-up young women and I would have my head in the *Sporting Globe*, reading about the Saturday football games.

That was still pretty much my routine while in Adelaide preparing for the 1960 Olympic Games. It was decided the Australian team would play in the local Adelaide competition, which was a decent initiative, and the North Adelaide club was designated to host the players from out of town. Players were billeted with families and young couples, and social events were arranged to break up the monotony of playing, training and working whatever jobs were available. At one of the social get-togethers, one of the young ladies managed to momentarily draw my interest away from the *Sporting Globe*. Her name was Margaret Nation and we have basically been together from that day to now, 60 years and counting.

I was extraordinarily lucky to marry Margaret. Probably the best decision of my life. I'm not sure she would return the compliment, but I knew better than to let her get away. Not that I was out there playing the field. Quite the opposite. Prior to marriage, my romantic conquests were quite few and rather forgettable.

As a teenager, I would go away with a group of friends to Warrnambool or Lakes Entrance over Christmas. We would go to local dances and a few of our group made connections that became permanent. But I never really even cracked it for something you would call a connection. I found out after one trip away that one of the girls asked a mate about my attitude towards women given I seemed to offer some attention, but also remain at arm's length. Clearly, I showed a little more attention to Margaret than to anyone else.

After initially getting to know each other in Adelaide, Margaret and I corresponded via letters while I was in Europe and Rome for the Olympics. The only drawback was it being snail mail, so most of the letters didn't arrive until I was back in Melbourne. Nonetheless, I received a note from Margaret saying she was moving to Melbourne to work in a shop owned by her aunty and uncle in the bayside suburb of Chelsea. But given my irregular hours with working, playing and coaching, and Chelsea being 30 kilometres away, it was still not a simple situation. So I got Margaret a job working in the canteen at the Albert Park Stadium with my mum, and with that I said to her, 'We might as well get married'. Very romantic.

On her acceptance of my marriage proposal, I warned Margaret that it would not be a normal lifestyle because of my work hours along with playing and coaching. She has since reminded me it took 30 years to have something even close to a normal lifestyle with meals at regular hours. For many of those 30 years, I was thankful for the invention of the microwave oven, so I could quickly heat my dinner at 10.30 after a full night of looking after Albert Park or having meetings or coaching engagements. It was impossible to do anything that was conventional, but I have to admit I have been incredibly lucky with the woman I married and spent my life with.

Right throughout our marriage, I have not been what anyone would seriously consider a good husband. With playing, coaching and work, I was regularly out of the house for 14 to 16 hours a day, seven days a week, even over the Christmas period. I was often away for days and weeks at a time, travelling overseas with teams or for meetings, which meant Margaret was at home with the kids and all the responsibilities that entailed.

Nor was I present for the births of either of our children, Janet and Andrew. Fittingly, when Andrew was born, I was in Adelaide for a national championship or similar event. So Margaret took a taxi to the hospital and I received news of Andrew's arrival second-hand. Being somewhat old-fashioned and from my generation, I didn't believe I would be any value in the maternity ward, anyway.

While I have tried to be a good father, Margaret has been more than a great mother and she has raised and shaped two extraordinary people. Our kids have inherited her compassion, her love and her empathy. Janet, in particular, is like Margaret with her care for people and animals. She will take home an injured sparrow and help an old lady over the street purely because it is the right thing to do. That is a quality she inherited from her mother. On the contrary, I have been known, particularly on the basketball court, to take the stance that you never give a sucker an even break.

Even though we are both now getting close to an age where we might need help to exist, Margaret still goes out of her way to help others, volunteering once a fortnight to take an elderly lady shopping. Which was how Margaret got connected with two ladies, one now 101 and the other 90, and they meet weekly for coffee and a chat at Chadstone Shopping Centre. It is fair to say the three are now firm friends and look forward to their catch-ups as much as anything.

Given the selfish nature of my basketball career and life, Margaret deserves every iota of enjoyment from life and what is now our extended family with seven grandchildren – four children for Andrew and three for Janet. Each of them has their own separate personality and each of them gets their own special attention from their grandmother.

Funnily enough, I can remember almost everyone's birthdates, except Janet and Andrew. I don't know why. One of life's unexplainable mysteries. I don't even remember my own birthdate. But I do remember the day before – August 15 – because it is VP Day, Victory in the Pacific to essentially mark the end of World War II. Then again, I'm not really big on celebrating birthdays, especially my own. Age is just a number and I don't really care how old I am.

While I might have needed prodding to remember their birthdays, the most important thing for me when it came to Janet and Andrew was for them to have good educations. We considered the possibility of sending them to private schools, if only for the last couple of years of secondary education. But the state school system served them both very well.

When it came to school, Janet was more serious and studious than Andrew, and her results were better. Janet went on from high school and achieved a diploma in sport and recreation and then completed a university degree. By contrast, Andrew's primary

school report cards were fairly repetitive: 'Progressing well …
Tends to be distracted in class … Needs to concentrate more.'

By the time Andrew got to university, it took him more than a
decade to graduate, regularly applying for exemptions and exten-
sions because of the many interruptions with basketball. In my
day, if you missed or failed a subject, you were gone. But Andrew
became Victoria University's model for the notion that if you
commit to getting a degree, the institution will help you get it. In
the end, we were all incredibly proud of the fact Andrew finally
graduated.

Over the years, I have often been asked about Janet's and
Andrew's involvement in basketball, and my answer has always
been the same: they were never pushed into playing. Of course,
they grew up with nine basketball courts tacked onto their house.
But they also had immediate access to table tennis, badminton,
squash, running, rowing, tennis, golf, football, cycling and whatever other activities were available in the Albert Park precinct.
Andrew tried football, we played tennis together and he would
have a hit of badminton. But I think he only really went to the
badminton hall for the food available at the canteen.

As for influence over Janet and Andrew playing basketball,
they were essentially left to their own devices and motivations.
I would sometimes offer advice and nothing more. I didn't coach
any of Andrew's teams until he was at the Under-16 or Under-18
level, but he had very good junior coaches who taught him well. I
did try to stay hands-off and give Andrew space to deal with his
trials and tribulations. Margaret did the same, albeit as Andrew's
most ardent supporter. While she would be a silent spectator at

games, woe betide any individual who said or did anything negative towards Andrew. They were immediately condemned for life. As good a human being as she is, Margaret can hold a grudge for a very long time when it comes to those who cross her children.

Which is what has made Margaret such a perfect wife and mother. She has been protective, loving, giving, sharing, guiding, selfless, providing and, perhaps more than anything, patient. How else would she have put up with me for 60 years and counting?

FLIPPING AND RENOVATING

It would seem that after a lifetime in basketball, any other career option was not an option. In some ways that is true. I was fortunate the job as Albert Park Stadium manager and playing for and coaching the Melbourne Tigers started and kept me in the basketball option for 50 years. But if things had turned out differently – if there had been a sliding-doors moment – my career path may have been vastly different and based in property.

Often on the lookout for somewhere to live and a way to make some money, my mother had a knack for the property game. In fact, she broke the mould given buying, renovating and selling houses was very much a male domain in the 1950s. But she was pretty good at it, and I was her on-site handyman as we converted derelict properties into habitable, and re-sellable, houses.

We never had any money, but banks would provide a loan on a small deposit. The first house Mum bought was in South Yarra and it cost the princely sum of 850 pounds. It doesn't sound much, but it was a fortune for us. It was a weatherboard house on a decent block of land, but the place was absolutely ramshackle. Floorboards were missing from the so-called loungeroom, so you could see the dirt below and the daily deposits of the tenant's pet. There were faeces along the walls, the oven had a tray overloaded with cooking fat. No wonder we got the place at such a cheap rate. We didn't live in it, but had trouble removing the tenants, and eventually had to buy them out.

My spare time after school was dedicated to renovating the house in South Yarra, and it was probably the greatest job of deceptive patch-up you could ever imagine. The door jambs were riddled with boring pests and other horrors, and that was just a small part of it. I would mix putty and linseed oil, fill the holes and smooth them out. Same with the walls. I would use a large sponge and plaster to cover the cracks, and every piece of work was done on a shoestring budget. Although, describing it as a shoestring is being generous. We cleaned it up, made it presentable and sold it for double our buying price in a fairly short time. It got us going on the property ladder and got mum on her feet financially.

As a woman, Mum was seen as an easy target by some real estate agents. They did not pick their mark well. We sold that South Yarra house privately, without the help of an agent. We advertised it in the newspaper and several agents called around, wanting to sell it on our behalf. We declined all offers. But when it was sold, one agent called in asking for his commission. We advised him to find the front door and keep walking. We both knew it was a con.

In reality, the business of renovating and selling houses was about learning on the go, from how to plaster to how to get the most money from a sale. Every house brought a new experience and lesson. The second house my mother bought was one of a pair. It was solid brick with the kitchen, bathroom and laundry all in the same location at the back of the house. With the plumbing all in one spot, we decided to add an extension as a separate bathroom. So I built the frame, which had to pass a council inspection before going further. The inspector came on site, looked at the frame and said, 'Where did you get this shitty timber? It's lousy'. I had no idea. We just bought the cheapest material, but he passed it anyway.

I would try to read about the skills and methods needed for renovating: plastering, carpentry, brickwork, moving fireplaces, knocking down walls and chimneys. But most of it was very much trial-and-error as the renovations were taking place and the evidence was there to see. We were renovating a property on the Nepean Highway, near North Road, Brighton, and I was plastering the walls as best I could for a rookie tradesman. There was a pub over the road that had cheap lunches, so I would go there to eat. One day I was in the pub and a bloke asked if I was plastering. The messy evidence on my overalls and arms suggested that to be the case. He said he could get me a job as a plasterer if I wanted one. I politely declined, pretty sure I wouldn't pass whatever test was needed.

Following my mother up the property ladder was a logical progression, but not to the same extent of buying, renovating and selling. The first investment property I bought was in Doncaster. It was an easy transaction: I looked at it and paid a deposit. I don't think I ever did anything to it and probably had the same tenants for 10 years. When the tenants moved out, I sold the property and got more than double what I paid for it.

Location was never an issue with investment properties, but sometimes there were hurdles to jump, especially when it came to other people's money. While we were living at Albert Park Stadium, I bought a place at Upwey in the Dandenong Ranges. It was a weatherboard house on a good block, but it was suffocating under a wild growth of blackberries. We got it cleaned up, painted it, installed a septic tank and got rid of the hippie tenants. The problem came after sale. The vendor had gone to Israel and died, prompting a dispute over his estate. A relative of the vendor reckoned the real estate agent and I colluded on the sale price, a false claim that took nine months to resolve.

Living in the cottage at Albert Park meant owning a house for my own family was never an urgent priority. But as our children, Janet and Andrew, got older, they were outgrowing the cottage and needed something a bit more conventional. We bought a place in the centre of what is known as St Kilda's Black Rectangle, not an ideal location for a family given the area's seedy reputation at the time. It was the mid-to-late 1970s and we paid about $44,000 for the property, which featured a house and six bungalows in the backyard. We started stripping the property and demolishing the bungalows, and an electrician mate named Barry was helping. I turned up one Sunday morning and the front door was open. I yelled out to Barry, thinking he was inside working. No answer. Then as I looked around, I noticed the front door and every other door was missing. Fireplaces and valuable fittings were gone. Marauders had been through and stripped the place.

Success in the property market can come down to the situation of being in the right place at the right time. After quickly getting rid of the house in the Black Rectangle, we looked at a double-storied mansion around the corner, but the $5,000 over my budget was too much. We made a bid on a house a couple of streets away and just missed out at auction. I had gone overseas, and Margaret called to say the agent wanted to know if we were still interested. I told her, yes, but we would only buy at the price of my final bid. They accepted the bid and we got ready to start some renovation work.

We had only taken over the property for about a fortnight when I got a phone call asking if I had bought the house at Gurner Street. When I confirmed that, the caller told me to get down there ASAP because people were moving in. 'What?!' I raced down there from Albert Park to see what was going on. There was nobody about, but the front door had been nailed shut. I went down the side and climbed through a window to find stuff everywhere. There were suitcases and clothes and goods and a note, declaring: 'Tenants' rights. Keep out.' Squatters had decided this was as good a house as any to occupy. I prised open the front door and started chucking all the squatters' gear out into the front yard. One of the squatters returned and asked what I was doing. When I informed him that he was moving out, he asked if I could wait until 4pm. You can guess my answer.

Just as we got the squatters out the door and started cleaning and renovating, there was a knock on the door. It was an estate agent saying local property was in real demand. He asked if I was interested in selling. The agent had very keen buyers and the only caveat was to immediately stop renovating. That suited me and we sold the house for a good profit.

When Margaret and I started to think about retiring, we didn't have any money, at least in terms of cash. So we decided to sell the house we had in St Kilda and downsize. That would leave us with some money to get by doing whatever we were going to do. We had two places in mind, one of them in Caulfield North that we now happily call home with the nameplate of *Geranium* for the birthplace of my mother. The agent had asked if we would bid at auction and we intended to. On the Thursday before the Saturday auction, the agent asked if we would go higher than our intended limit. We said no and that we were looking at another place just as good. The agent sold it to us on the spot before auction. The local newspaper reported the sale and described it as 'the unliveable property' in Arthur Street.

When we bought the property, it was basically a boarding house for university students. The owner lived out the back in a granny flat, leaving the house to the students. It did need a bit of work and it is now a wonderful house. Margaret says it's become too big, but we are settled, and it is in a fantastic location. Of course, location is one of the keys to being successful in the property market. But it was more about the right price when my mum started flipping houses, and that has been the same for me, given my salary as a basketball administrator was always at the lower end of the scale. I am not complaining about that at all. I was doing a job I loved in a sport I loved. But without the spare time to renovate houses and make some money, I would have been in deep strife.

Who knows? If I had gone into the property game instead of basketball administration and coaching, I would certainly have been a lot wealthier. But that money could not replace or match the value of the rich experiences I have banked from basketball.

BACKYARD BUSINESS

One of the major side benefits of touring overseas with Australia and Melbourne Tigers was the shopping not available at home. Not department store shopping. Basketball shopping: the latest shoes, balls, clothing that were readily available, especially in the United States, but not in Australia, especially during the 1960s and 1970s.

It was not unusual for me and the other players to return home with enough gear to open our own shop, stocking up especially on shoes and balls, and we would get them by any means necessary. It is easy to take the quality of basketballs for granted these days, but during the 1960s and 1970s we often used balls from China that were cheap and not of the highest quality. Even at the 1960 Olympics, FIBA – basketball's world governing body – opted to use a ball that was panelled and stitched together. It was like a soccer ball, making it almost impossible to dribble without taking your eyes off the ball for fear it would take an awkward bounce. It was a nightmare for the point guards, who need to be able to see every player on the court and know the ball will return to their hands when dribbling.

Getting basketballs of quality was one of Ken Watson's priorities if we were to make our players better. On one US tour, Ken went to a factory and did a deal for some balls. They were deflated and handed out among the players to stow in their luggage for the return flight home, thus avoiding import taxes and freight costs.

To get the best gear in the developing era of Australian basketball, it wasn't so much a case of beg, borrow or steal. But it was close.

During the 1964 Olympics, I became friendly with Larry Brown, a guard on the US team that won the gold medal. Larry would go on to be considered one of the game's greatest – and most-travelled – coaches, leading a total of 13 teams across the American Basketball Association (ABA), National Basketball Association (NBA) and college. After a tournament, it was common to swap uniforms or warm-up gear with opponents, which I did with Larry. But I definitely got the better end of the deal. Whatever I gave him, it did not compare to the Converse shoes I received, basically brand new after being issued pre-tournament. Having shoes of that quality was not common in Australia, nor were there too many basketball-specific shoes on the market. I had tried wearing boxing boots at one stage, but the soles simply did not have a good enough grip.

On every trip to the US, I was impressed by the uniforms worn by the opposition, along with the T-shirts and warm-up tops that were readily available for fans as well as players. I knew there had to be a way to get basketball shoes and uniforms of quality and quantity in Australia. So, with the unbelievable hard work of my mother, we started up our own business of making uniforms for teams in Melbourne and throughout Australia. Essentially, it was your typical backyard business with my mother cutting and sewing the uniforms, and me spreading word about the uniforms to anyone I could.

As it turned out, some of those shirts and jerseys I had swapped at the Olympics and world championship were cut up and turned into sample swatches as we tried to source the best material at the cheapest rates. That inevitably sent us to Asia, where we were ably guided and helped by our friends and associates George Foo and Yemin Sung. They would supply our material, provide valuable advice and point us in the right direction for what we needed.

One thing Yemin or George could not help with was a flock printing machine, enabling us to produce T-shirts and warm-up tops similar to the American teams. It was easy to copy the patterns and the styling of the lettering and numbering for the screen-printing. The problem was the flock printing so we could have more than one colour of letters or numbers on tops. I had researched suppliers in the US, but it was too expensive to import a machine. So, as the Gazes have done for much of their lives, we set about making our own flocking machine.

It was certainly not high-tech or state-of-the-art. I had been able to locate an electrostatic machine and a supplier of flock, the key adhesive in making the process work. I took a drawer from an old desk and replaced the bottom with a sheet of fine copper mesh, attached a cable to the electrostatic machine, and hooked an earth wire onto a length of steel that went under the drawer/ flock printer. The final touch in the process was putting the shirts under heat lamps, homemade, of course.

With that, we started producing T-shirts and windcheaters with logos and mascots of American college teams. The use of the logos and mascots was probably illegal, but the knowledge and adherence of copyright laws in that area was basically zero in those days. Plus there was minimal chance of the National Collegiate Athletic Association (NCAA) or a university coming after the Gaze cottage industry. That said, the business was not so much about making a dollar as it was about providing a service for clubs looking to upgrade their uniforms and improve their image.

Similarly, I branched out into the shoe business, trying to get decent basketball footwear at a good price. The taxes applied to bringing in a bulk shipment of shoes from the US were prohibitive, so again we looked to Asia and a mate in the Philippines. He did not supply us with canvas Converse shoes, but they were a direct copy of the famous brand. They were named FRCs, and on one trip I brought back about 20 pairs. Coming through customs at the airport, I was sure there would be some serious questioning. The customs officers were sceptical when I told them they were all for private use, but I got through. Had they bothered to check them closely, they would have discovered a range of sizes and I would have been busted.

After that initial haul of 20, we started importing in the more traditional method with bulk orders to keep a good stock at the shop we had established inside the Albert Park stadium. The only real drawback was they did not manufacture the shoes in any sizes bigger than 10, which tended to rule out a fair portion of the Australian basketball community. But we did well with the shoes and they were popular until commercial outlets started to expand and sell more mainstream and authentic basketball apparel.

On one tour to China, I had time to visit Yemin in Hong Kong for a couple of days. Our business at home was doing well and Yemin wanted to know why I had continued to stay in coaching and administration and not develop the business into something bigger and highly profitable. I guess I had a small entrepreneurial streak, but not the desire to go all-in on business and leave behind the love of the game.

The uniform business in the 1970s had unlimited scope in Australia and I tried to convince our club and state association directors to take over the business. They declined, the business faded, and it was a major opportunity lost for the sport. Those who subsequently got into the uniform business became millionaires, and good luck to them for taking a chance and working hard to reap the benefits. Maybe my vision was fanciful, but basketball in Victoria had a chance to develop a major, self-sustaining revenue stream and it didn't happen.

Either way, the backyard business served its purpose and I am eternally grateful to my mother for her work. She might be considered something of a pioneer in Australian basketball for her work with the sewing machine, and helped move us away from the days of beg, borrow or steal.

A COTTAGE BY THE LAKE

Clad only in pyjamas and running barefoot through the con-
fines of Albert Park in the middle of the night might sound like
enough evidence to have me certified. At times, I would not disagree. Except this was in the name of truth, justice and ... Well,
actually, I was chasing a bandit making off with some item pil-
laged from the old stadium, an occurrence that happened several
times over the years.

As the live-in caretaker at Albert Park Stadium, the job
description was all-encompassing from opening the doors in the
morning to locking them at night, and everything in between and
after, given thieves did not work regular hours. Living in the cottage attached to the stadium basically made my job a 24/7/365
role that was more a lifestyle than anything else. In fact, while the
money was ordinary, I could not have had a better job given what
it allowed my family and me to do with basketball, right down to
chasing crooks out of the place.

If there has been an age-old problem for basketball in Australia
– especially in Victoria and Melbourne – it has been a lack of courts
and suitable venues. It was a problem when the sport started here,
and it continues to be a problem today as basketball and the number
of players outgrows the facilities. At least now the kids play in pal-
aces relative to the cramped church and army drill halls we once
played in. Some of those venues were not even big enough to put a
court in, so the sidelines and/or baselines were halfway up the wall.
It was a brave man who chased a loose ball in those days.

As always, Ken Watson worked tirelessly to get better venues and courts around Melbourne. When I first met Ken, the Victorian Basketball Association (VBA) games were played at the Melbourne Showgrounds in Flemington on Wednesday nights. The lower grades were in the dog pavilion with a sloping floor, and the State Championship games were played in a larger hall. In essence, they were nothing more than glorified tin sheds, and the term glorified is being generous.

With the 1956 Olympic Games staged in Melbourne, there was hope for basketball to get a quality, dedicated, multi-court home. Part of the Olympic charter is that there must be a legacy after the Games. Athletics and soccer got Olympic Park, swimming got what became known as the Glasshouse, and other sports benefitted too. Basketball got nothing. The 1956 Olympic tournament was played at the Royal Exhibition Building, which meant nothing had been built specifically for basketball. The eventual legacy was that we used the timber flooring from the courts at the Royal Exhibition Building to build the tiered seating at Albert Park.

After much lobbying and agitating post-1956, basketball, badminton, squash and table tennis found homes on the shores of Albert Park Lake. Much thanks for that goes to Senator Pat Kennelly, the chairman of the Albert Park Trust, for his work and wisdom. While Ken Watson was close to sealing a deal for a two-court venue in Northcote, Senator Kennelly made an offer that was too good to refuse – a six-court stadium at Albert Park.

During World War II, the military used three large warehouses at Albert Park for storage, later passing them to the Federal

Government to garage vehicles. The vision of Senator Kennelly was to convert these warehouses into sporting facilities, including one for basketball. The first, and most important, aspect in the project was to raise the funds necessary. As was his way, Ken, as VBA secretary, grabbed the opportunity with both hands, persuaded his fellow administrators to back it and then formed a co-op to generate the money needed for basketball's part of the project. The various basketball associations of the time contributed, and each was awarded a night of play at the new stadium, an order that still stands.

Where I came into the frame was via another of Ken's initiatives. Or maybe I just happened to be at a loose end, and he grabbed it. After approval for the stadium was given, the next step was to appoint a manager, even though nobody had much clue about a detailed job description. As Ken described it, manage the business and grow the sport. It wasn't exactly an attractive or enticing job pitch, but the timing was the most advantageous aspect for Ken.

At that stage, I was studying engineering, playing football and basketball and using the rest of my time to flip houses with my mother – buy one, refurbish it, sell it, repeat. When considering Ken's job offer, I figured that basketball was played at night so I could still study, play football and basketball and still have time to do the houses on the weekends. So I accepted the job. It did not take long to find out my theory of continuing my various activities was totally wrong.

In some regards, I was actually the project manager for the conversion of the warehouse to the six-court basketball stadium, so I was on site full-time. While the workers constructed the stadium, I set to work on the former canteen that had serviced the warehouse employees and turned it into a cottage for my mother and me. It was three rooms and a toilet, so I created two bedrooms and kitchen-living area. It was modest, but it was home for me and mum. It was safe and it was out of the way. The only disturbances were some possums on the roof and the noise of amorous couples, parking their cars next to the cottage believing they had complete privacy.

In time, when two more courts were added at the end of the complex, a small brick cottage was built between the basketball and badminton stadiums, and that became home for me, Margaret, Janet and Andrew.

But the increases in stadium size required upgrading the insurance, and that brought inconvenience and comedic adventures. The insurance policy to cover the expanded venue required an automatic alarm system for the stadium. If there was an intruder, the alarm would trip in the security firm's office and would sound in the stadium. More often than not, an alarm at 1.30am was false and I could call security to tell them not to bother attending. Then there were times when intruders got in and out and the alarm system failed completely.

Occasionally, the alarm operated correctly, and I could be on the scene within a minute rather than wait for security to turn up. One such time, I was roused by the alarm, pulled on a pair of tracksuit pants and wandered into the main court area, assuming I was dealing with another false call. I still had to negotiate the dark to get to the switchboard to flick on the lights, and I sensed I should arm myself. The only thing handy was a metal pipe about 20cm long, so I grabbed it and headed for the switchboard. As I was about to hit the switch, there was banging and crashing and a shadowy figure flashed past me, heading for the back of the stadium. I flicked on the lights, saw the front door had been smashed, and gave chase.

The next scene would not have been out of place in a *Keystone Cops* movie. While there was a row of seats between me and the would-be burglar, I was sure I could block his escape. After a few cat-and-mouse moves and me brandishing my 20cm metal pipe, he tried to broker peace. In a thick European accent, he said: 'You stop, I give you 50 quid.' With several adjectives and obscenities thrown in, I advised the intruder where he could put the 50 quid. His next move gave pause for thought, pulling out a screwdriver that was about 30cm long and sharpened to a point. Despite that, I tried to jump over the seating to apprehend him, but he made good his escape, crashing through the double doors near the cottage and producing a blood-curdling scream from Margaret. She told me later she didn't know who was coming out first, him or me. By now, I wasn't sure if there was more than one bandit. One, I thought, may have left via the front door and returned to support his mate and Margaret was screaming at him. I paused long enough to ensure Margaret was safe and for the bandit to scale the back fence. I continued the chase to the back fence, only to see the intruder well on his way to Queens Road and a clean getaway.

As extra security, we had a Blue Heeler – *Corina*. She was a perfect family pet and guard dog and was always protective of me when we jogged around the lake. One night when the alarm sounded, *Corina* and I went to investigate. It turned out a teenager – probably about 16 years old – had broken into the stadium sports store through the roof. As he was nonchalantly trying on a tracksuit top, I grabbed the keys to unlock the store. I had him cold and took a calm approach. Perhaps too calm. I intended to take him to the office and wait there until the police arrived. As we left the store, I was about to go left when he went right and made a run for it. I yelled to *Corina* to give chase, bark, do anything. She just sat and watched.

Determined to recapture the intruder, I gave chase, running around the front of the stadium and down towards the lake and the golf course. It was about this time, after a few hundred metres, that I realised I was barefooted and running on a surface of crushed rock and pebble. It was like running on broken glass. I slowed, not wanting to be sprinting down Queens Road in my bed attire. The thief kept running and was gone in the darkness. Nothing was lost except some of my pride. On neither occasion were the police able to make an arrest, and I just had to put it down as an occupational hazard.

The saddest and most serious alarm was not tripped by a burglar. It was caused by fire, not that the security company alerted me to the fact. By now, we were living off site and had moved to a house in St Kilda. I got a phone call one night in 1987 to inform me Albert Park Stadium was on fire, perhaps caused by a faulty television set in the referees' room. I arrived to see the office and administration area had been destroyed, but the fire officers had done a great job to limit the damage to the basketball courts. While some of the backboards had melted, the floors had only been scorched and competition continued almost uninterrupted except for the bitterly cold winds coming off the lake. The length of the stadium was sealed only by wire mesh until re-construction took place and we shifted the administration into portable huts.

The basketball and business communities rallied immediately to supply the VBA with new office equipment, furniture and supplies, making our recovery much quicker and smoother than it might have been. Unfortunately, what could not be replaced were the years of records, historic documents and memorabilia that were kept at the office. It was irreplaceable and heart breaking to know it was now a pile of ashes.

The push to get basketball its own true home, complete with an international-standard arena has been long, hard and unfruitful. It was plainly obvious that Albert Park would outgrow its usefulness, and the efforts of Victoria's many basketball administrators and volunteers over time has been unstinting. Melbourne's National Basketball League (NBL) teams moved from Albert Park and their suburban homes to the Glasshouse and then to Melbourne Park, paying exorbitant hire costs along the way. But we needed a home for big games and mid-week battlers, and every proposed project always had a spoiler, usually political.

There was a proposal from Channel 0 (now Channel 10) to convert the badminton stadium at Albert Park into a 5000-seat venue. There was an opportunity to convert the Millers Rope Works site in Brunswick into a basketball hub. There was a proposal for a sports precinct in Thornbury. There was a plan for a site in the Chapel Street shopping area with a venue to be surrounded by shops, cafes and restaurants. All of them had some level of support until it got to crunch time, and when the councils and politicians crunched their numbers, their support disappeared.

Even when we did get a new venue to replace the Albert Park Stadium, basketball – frankly – again got screwed. The only politician who supported the notion that basketball deserved its own international-standard facility was John Cain, Premier of Victoria from 1982 to 1990. With Melbourne's bid for the 1996 Olympic Games, it seemed Premier Cain would help basketball get what it needed and wanted. But that chance was killed when Atlanta got the 1996 Games and Sydney got the 2000 Olympics. Despite that, Premier Cain announced a joint venture, involving public and government funding, but it did not have enough legs.

Almost in desperation, the sporting bodies from the Albert Park precinct collaborated on a project to redevelop our venues and build one 5000-seat venue for all to use. The cost was estimated at $15 million, most of it coming from the sports, but with help from the government. We made a strong presentation to the government, seeking support, and felt we had a very good chance of success. But before we could even get our hopes up, the government hit us with a blindside punch. The Formula 1 Grand Prix was moving from Adelaide to Melbourne – more precisely to Albert Park – from 1996. As such, the old Albert Park sports venues would be torn down and replaced by a new multi-purpose venue: Melbourne Sports and Aquatic Centre (MSAC), with the emphasis on aquatic as the government felt the need for an international-class swimming pool. It was quickly pointed out the MSAC pool was expensive given the entire project was going to cost $65 million, but every sport except swimming could have had new venues for just $15 million. Nor did it take time for the government to land the knockout blow, announcing the planned 5000-seat arena at MSAC would be reduced to 2000 seats.

The first games at the old Albert Park Stadium were played in 1958, and the official opening was marked by a game between Victoria and the American Mormons. The final game at the venue was in 1997 between Melbourne Tigers and the University of Arizona, coached by the legendary Lute Olson. The main court at the old place was packed that night, standing room only as a fitting farewell. The atmosphere and buzz that night captured exactly what Albert Park was like. The seats were right on top of the court, the fans could see everything happening on the floor and the players could feel the fans and their emotions more than anywhere else. Even though the main court only held little more than 1000 people, the atmosphere was better than some of the more modern arenas with 5000 people in the seats.

In fact, Albert Park hosted some major games over its history, including the very first NBL grand final in 1979. It also gave birth to many successful teams and individual careers and created some legends along the way. If you want to use a cliché, Albert Park was the Mecca of Australian basketball, drawing the best of the best from around the nation. Indeed, even the pick-up games were worth watching and became something of a phenomenon of their own.

Every Friday afternoon, the best players in Melbourne would gather at Albert Park for what became known as *Jungle Ball*. In other words, there wasn't much structure and the rules were loose. It was what we know today as street ball. The first 10 players to arrive were divided into two teams, games were usually first to 10 baskets, and the winning team stayed on the floor. At the end of it all, the only thing at stake was manly pride, which meant things got serious and heated, sometimes to the point of boiling over. Such as the time one aggrieved player stormed off the court, went to the locker room, returned with a knife and stabbed his opponent. Police were called, charges were laid and by the next Friday, *Jungle Ball* was back like nothing had happened.

The fondest memories of Albert Park are as much about the people as the games and the structure itself. After all, Albert Park was the home for the VBA offices, and inside those offices were some of the greatest people you could ever meet and work with. All of them were devoted and committed to basketball, whether they were paid employees or salt-of-the-earth volunteers.

Between 1931, when the VBA was formed, and 1997, there were only five presidents of the governing body. The first was Alan Hughes, a mild-mannered man with a brilliant legal mind. He was followed by equally mild-mannered Percy Foster, a tireless worker in youth services. Percy was succeeded by Jack Carter, an astute businessman, shortly after the opening of the Albert Park Stadium in 1959.

Next came Malcolm Speed, who had made the playing step from Church of England Boys Society in Balwyn to Melbourne Tigers. A fierce competitor, Mal stepped away from top-level basketball to focus on his law studies before returning as an administrator. To say the least, Mal was ambitious and introduced administration reforms and set high goals for the sport. Having achieved those goals, Mal became chairman of the NBL, leading the organisation through the transition from amateur competition to professional league.

Another former Tigers player, John Maddock, followed Mal as VBA president. An Olympian and astute negotiator, John had a prominent career in education, guiding Box Hill TAFE to a leading role in the tertiary system. Not surprisingly, John also moved on and became chairman of Basketball Australia.

The task of trying to fund and build basketball stadia and facilities has never been easy, despite the amazing work done by Ken Watson and others. Ken established the Victorian Amateur Basketball Association Co-operative Society to generate funds for the construction of Albert Park and other venues. Jack Carter had a term as co-op chairman and was followed by Henry Cooper, a very smart engineer and administrator.

I am forever indebted to all these men who had equal passion for the progress of the sport and for their patience and wisdom. I can't remember ever having harsh words or serious disputes with any of them.

The people who really made things tick were our staff at Albert Park. After being the *Lone Ranger* for a while, the first person we hired was Lorraine *Dutchy* Cooke. We shared the office space, but more often than not *Dutchy* was out changing nets on the rings, mending equipment, or collecting entry fees at the door.

With the opportunity to grow our staff, we usually hired people from within basketball, and the dedication and commitment to the sport was clear. It was interesting to observe the passing parade of staff members who grew up in the sport, married others from within the sport and raised families in the sport. A prime example was Sandra McPherson, who followed *Dutchy* as my so-called secretary and managed to do much of my work while I was out lobbying politicians or finding sponsors. In fact, Sandra became so busy she actually hired Jan Lienert to be her assistant. Those names might not mean anything to many because most people would know them as Sandra Tomlinson and Jan Smithwick.

It was interesting to observe the office dynamic as both were outstanding players, representing Australia at the world championship. Sandra played for Telstars, one of the top teams in the state championship, while Jan played for Comets, their main rivals. Fortunately, both were great friends and have remained so, teaming up for the Masters Games every year. Along the way, Sandra married Ray Tomlinson, an Olympian and one of our Melbourne Tigers stars, while Jan married Rob Smithwick, a smart guard with Coburg Giants. Without the loyal and consistent support of Sandra and Jan – and all the VBA staff – I could not have done my job.

The American influence at the VBA was manifold and chief among it was Bruce Case. Brought to Australia as a schoolteacher, Bruce was the VBA's first Director of Coaching and responsible for developing our Level 1, 2 and 3 coaching courses. The DOC role was assumed by another American, Bill Palmer. I finally got Bill to the VBA after I had unsuccessfully tried to sign him as a player for Melbourne Tigers. Bill also created our referee training courses, setting the standard for the rest of the country, before moving to the NBL as chief executive.

We didn't have Lee Iacocca, the car industry titan, on the staff at the VBA, but I kept in mind his line that 'a good manager needs a good bean counter'. Managers always want to do more and spend more, while the bean counters need to keep the reigns tight. In that regard, I need to make special mention of Maurie Pawsey, our treasurer when we built Albert Park, and his successor, Peter Bold. They were teammates on championship-winning YMCA teams and kept my spending in check enough to ensure surpluses for the VBA each year.

There are so many other people I need to thank and mention here, but it would be impossible to do so. To all those people who served, worked and played at Albert Park, know that my memories of you are still clear and I love you all.

As you can see, Albert Park was a home for basketball, basketballers and the basketball community. It was truly a home for the Gaze family, and one of the greatest places for Andrew and Janet to grown up. The six courts eventually became nine, and the little brick house down the side became *Pete's Bar*, frequented by many players after their games. Though the Albert Park stadium is long gone, the memories remain, and the old place still has a soft place in the hearts of many. Even better, I am no longer chasing would-be thieves in the middle of the night.

PART 2

The
Player

THE REAL GODFATHER

It was a bitterly cold Wednesday night, which is not unusual for Melbourne at any time of year. As a wiry kid, I didn't have much meat on the bones to keep me warm, a fact noticed by a man I only knew by sight. The man approached me and held out a wind-cheater, telling me to put it on because I looked cold.

That was my first interaction with Ken Watson, a man who had the most profound influence on my life. Personally, and in basketball, Ken was a surrogate father, mentor, example, and friend. I could not have had anyone better. As I soon and regularly observed, Ken didn't offer me that windcheater because I was special. He did that for everyone, especially helping young people and getting them involved in basketball. Ken did that until the day he died.

People have often described me as the godfather of Australian basketball. It is an inaccurate statement. Ken Watson was the real Godfather of Australian Basketball, and the capital letters are there on purpose. What Ken did for the game at all levels cannot be underestimated and will likely never be done by a single individual ever again.

Over his decades of devotion and service to basketball, Ken was a player, coach and administrator. But he was so much more. Ken basically formed Melbourne Tigers, introduced the Shuffle offence to Australia, and pioneered overseas tours for Australian club teams. Ken was secretary of the Australian Basketball Federation (now Basketball Australia) and the Victorian Basketball Association (now Basketball Victoria) - the latter for 40 years - and was instrumental in creating Victoria's elite junior leagues and the South East Conference (later known as the South East Australian Basketball League and now NBL1), competitions that have been taken for granted. A good player in his own right, Ken also coached the Tigers (known previously as Melbourne Church) and the Australian national team at the 1956 and 1968 Olympic Games.

Even while playing and coaching, Ken's priority always seemed to be the game and the growth of basketball, and he was almost the sole reason the sport in Victoria survived past World War II. With so many young men going to the battlefronts of Europe and Asia, Ken rallied as many boys as he could onto basketball courts through the Church of England Boys Society, encouraging other church groups to do the same. Ken progressed basketball in so many ways on and off the court, coaching and advising almost right up to the time of his death at the age of 88.

On that cold and bitter Wednesday night when I first met Ken, the Victorian State Championship games were played in one of the main halls at Melbourne Showgrounds. It was not an ideal venue, but was better than the lower grades, which played on a sloping asphalt surface in the dog pavilion. But Ken became a real driver behind improved facilities and the creation of the old Albert Park Stadium, which became home for Victorian basketball and me.

As a coach, Ken introduced the Shuffle offence that became the Tigers' staple forever after and oversaw success at state and national levels with the club. As coach, Ken led Victorian teams at the Australian Championship, perpetuating a serious rivalry with New South Wales that had started during his own playing days. As an undersized big man during the late 1940s, it was said the battles between Ken and Peter Mullins of NSW were legendary.

Those battles with Peter Mullins surely fuelled Ken's desire to beat NSW at every turn. The rivalry became so embedded within Ken that, before any Victoria-NSW encounter, he would tear off a piece of bark from the Separation Tree located in Melbourne's Royal Botanical Gardens. It was more than superstition – it was highly symbolic. The Separation Tree was where the citizens of Melbourne congregated on November 15, 1850 to celebrate the proclamation of Victoria becoming a colony separate from NSW.

Despite Ken's devotion and contribution to basketball, one of my early memories is that Ken's teams were always booed. Whatever fans were on site cheered for the opposition. I soon came to realise that Ken's teams were good, and as an administrator he came under unfair fire as an authority figure. It was and is something of an Australian trait and an attitude that has carried on through basketball history.

In the era before the whiteboard, Ken would carry a chunk of white chalk in his pocket. During a timeout he would diagram a play on the floor. It was a lesson I followed, although I didn't have the same access to copious amounts of chalk given Ken was a schoolteacher. I would make do with putting five coins on the floor, moving them around. More often than not, a player would interrupt to ask where the basket was.

Perhaps more than anything, Ken was totally humble and utterly selfless, and I was a major beneficiary of those innate qualities. Never more so than when Ken basically forced me into becoming head coach of the Tigers and the Australian national team, in the days before it was known as *the Boomers*.

There was no question Ken could have continued coaching the Tigers beyond 1970. He was only 50 but had an eye to the future and essentially would not take 'no' for an answer when he 'suggested' I take over as head coach. Similarly, he led the move for me to be named coach of the Australian team at around the same time, going from playing at the 1970 world championship to coaching at the 1972 Olympics.

I have so much to be thankful for when it comes to Ken Watson, but so do many, many others. Apart from the countless people he directly and indirectly helped through basketball, Ken was an amazing educator as a mathematics teacher at Swinburne Technical School.

What made Ken such a good teacher was his ability to make the complicated sound simple and be understood quite easily. One Friday night I noticed one of the Tigers junior players sitting up in the Albert Park bleachers surrounded by books and taking notes. I asked what he was doing, and he explained he was working on a school assignment. This kid was an A-grade student and had his educational future all planned. One night he mentioned he was struggling with maths. After a couple of tutorials with Ken, he was right back on track. Ken had made the complex problem into a solvable equation by way of simple explanation. It was not so much the method as it was the communication that was key in solving the problem.

Not surprisingly, Ken's family was neck-deep in basketball in almost every facet. Of his three sons – Ray, David and Ian – David was an NBL referee and long-time overseer of the Tigers boys' program, Ray played at the 1968 Olympics, and Ian was a two-time Olympian before dying of a cancer at the tragically young age of 31. But if there was a dynamo in the family, it was Ken's wife Betty, a legend of Australian women's basketball. Asked to organise a governing body for the female side of the sport, Ken basically handed the responsibility across the kitchen table to Betty. He could not have made a better decision as Betty became a driving force and amazing influence over decades, progressing women's basketball in Australia just as Ken had done for the men. Both were indefatigable when it came to basketball.

Coaching and teaching were in Ken's blood and he continued coaching the Tigers juniors into his 70s, and then coaching juniors in Geelong after he and Betty had moved to the coastal town of Aireys Inlet.

It was fascinating to watch Ken at trainings with his under-12 and under-14 players. He had them moving methodically, running patterns almost like little robots, and it was something of a mystery to most of us. But it worked and, because of Ken's extraordinary teaching skills he kept producing players of the future for the Tigers and, most importantly, for basketball.

Despite his experience and knowledge, Ken never really gave up on trying to learn more about basketball and unlock the secrets of the game. There was rarely a day Ken would not call me between classes at Swinburne Tech to talk about the game – or games – and he was always looking for the undefendable offence. Unfortunately, I don't think he ever found it before his coaching days were curtailed by age and the onset of Alzheimer's disease.

Having Ken as my coach was an amazingly fortunate occurrence because he was such an unbelievably good teacher. But I was even more fortunate to have Ken Watson in my life, starting from that bitterly cold Wednesday night when he made the kind gesture of handing me a windcheater to keep warm.

THE FIGHTING GAZES

It was generally considered among opposition teams that if they could get the Gaze brothers fighting and arguing among ourselves, they had a good chance of winning the game. It was a fair comment and probably something of a compliment. The three of us did tend to bicker during games, sometimes getting close to blows. But it probably also showed we were good enough that other teams needed us to self-destruct to have a chance of winning.

Not that Barry, Tony and I were instant basketball superstars. But we had a combination of skill, fitness, nous and ferocious competitiveness and that made our team, *Powerhouse*, pretty tough to beat. That combination of qualities was probably evident in our various fields of success during our lives. Whatever inherent abilities we had were enhanced by enquiring minds and the determination and persistence to reach the level we felt achievable in business, sport and life.

While I had a crack at ice hockey and gymnastics, they were too expensive for me, so football and tennis were my sports of choice as a young teenager. Basketball was introduced to me and Tony via Barry, who had been recruited by Geoff Swan, a World War II army officer whose bravery was mentioned in despatches. Working closely with Ken Watson, Geoff had used his military connections and influence to make army drill halls available for basketball games and training, and he was a key organiser and coach at *Powerhouse*.

It took about two years of badgering by Barry for Tony and me to eventually give in and attend a training session. In no time, we formed a team under the *Powerhouse* banner and played our first games at the Try Boys hall in South Yarra. At the time we didn't realise it, but the court was about two-thirds the size of a regulation court, and the better players could make shots from the centreline without too many problems. Other halls that hosted games were so small that halfway up the wall was out, and you had to have one foot touching the wall before making an inbounds pass. Another venue had such a low roof that any shots from further than 15 feet required the ball to go over and through the rafters.

The 1952 Australian Championship between state teams was played at the Royal Exhibition Building in Melbourne, and that was my first exposure to basketball at the top level. It was also the event that lit the fuse for me to start thinking that basketball might be worth pursuing to the highest possible levels. Two other significant influences in choosing that path were watching the 1956 Olympic tournament, also at the Exhibition Building, and being recruited by Ken Watson to play for his team, Church – from the Church of England Boys Society – which became Melbourne Tigers.

My brother Tony and a bloke who was to become a long-time teammate and lifetime friend, Bill Wyatt, were also recruited to play with Church as Ken started to develop a strong team. Along with YMCA, we were able to provide some strong competition and resistance to the Mormons, the best team in the State Championship and a real influence on basketball in Australia. With the 1956 Olympic Games set for Melbourne, the Church of

Latter Day Saints sent a group of top players – fulfilling their two-year missionary commitment – to Victoria with a twin objective: help the Australians (and others) prepare for the Olympics and use basketball to make it easier to spread word of their religion.

The team was led by player-coach DeLyle Condie, who had played at the University of Utah. He became a friend and con-fidante to Ken Watson, who was named coach of the Australian team for the 1956 Games. It was perfect timing for everyone. With advice from and conversations with DeLyle about the methods and innovations of US college basketball, Ken was able to share new knowledge and awareness with the national team. Most of all, though, the Mormons set a standard of play and sportsmanship that the rest of us could only aspire to.

The 1956 Olympics came too early in my basketball career to be a serious option as a player. I had just turned 20 and was still somewhat attached to football. But the Olympics did prove a serious turning point for my sporting career and life. I attended as many games as possible during the Olympic tournament, observing and absorbing how the best players in the world played the game. In truth, Australia really struggled at the Olympics given its minimal preparation and finished 12th of 15 teams with a 2-5 record. The United States, led by a pair of future Hall of Famers – Bill Russell and KC Jones – won the gold, beating the Soviet Union by 34 points in the final.

Even though I was a bit physically frail for football, I had been voted the best player of the Sunday League and was an automatic selection for Prahran in the Victorian Football Association. I was athletic enough for basketball, and Ken Watson's coaching helped me progress as a shooter. With his research into modern methods used in American college basketball at the time, Ken's instruction enabled Bill Wyatt and me to learn how to execute a jump shot. Until then, the standard moves in basketball were driving to the basket for a lay-up, a one-handed push shot, currently described as a *floater* from-mid range, and a two-handed set shot. We learned how to execute a jump shot by observing sequence photographs Ken had extracted from the American magazine called *Scholastic Coach*. The ability to score with jump shots from mid-range opportunities as Bill drove from right to left, and I drove from left to right, gave Ken some weapons that took some time for opposing teams to counter.

In the meantime, Ken upgraded and improved his strategies, including the development of the Shuffle offence. I embraced this more strategic element of the sport. I have often used the analogy of the great chess players who could visualise the moves two or three plays ahead of the game to compete more favourably against their opponents. I was not in the same category as the great chess players, but I was certainly a student of the game.

My first season with Ken Watson and Church was in 1955, losing the grand final to YMCA club Daina, which was comprised of Latvians who had migrated to Australia. Among them was Peter Bumbers, who I still consider to be one of the best shooters Australian basketball has ever seen. He had what I referred to as a no-jump jump shot, but he could be unstoppable, getting most of his scoring from around the top of the keyway after getting rid of his defender with a quick fake. During one game for Victoria at the Australian Championship in Hobart, Peter scored 50 points, missing only one shot. Remember, this is 30 years before the introduction of the three-point line, so all his baskets were twos and free-throws.

Also of note from that 1955 season were three of my Church teammates: John Raschke, Peter Demos and Bill Wyatt. Originally from Newcastle and finishing his medical degree at the University of Melbourne, John was to become prominent in several aspects of basketball, particularly coaching Australia at the 1970 world championship and as a key instigator in the formation of the National Basketball League. A migrant from Greece, Peter played for Australia at the 1956 Olympics and had a charismatic, enthusiastic and flashy style of play, but he also took time to offer me guidance that I truly valued and appreciated. One of the first Australians to master the jump shot, Bill was an excellent player and he and I became a pair when we were on the floor together. It was Gaze and Wyatt, Wyatt and Gaze. Didn't matter which way you looked at it.

With the state championship a rising level for the best players, the next step was to make the Victorian team. That happened for me for the first time in 1957, when the Australian Championship was staged at the Royal Exhibition Building on the same court that hosted the Olympics Games the year before. I got to experience first-hand the power of South Australia and its group of excellent players that included George Dancis, Inga Freidenfelds, Tom Tiliks, Algy Ignatavicius and Andras Eiler. Those five players were from eastern Europe, part of the crop of talent from countries like Latvia, Hungary, Estonia, Lithuania and Bulgaria that made a huge contribution to Australian basketball. Other players of note to come from South Australia and its migrant roots were John and Les Hody, Mike Dancis, Werner Linde, Andy Blicavs and Huba Nagy, but those other guys got things going in the 1950s. As it turned out, I shared the court with some of those players on the national team when I was chosen for the 1960 Olympics, a situation that left a profound impact on me and cemented my friendship with Bill Wyatt.

In the meantime, life with Church continued almost seamlessly as we continued to make grand finals and win titles. There was no longer a chance for opponents to get the Gaze brothers arguing in the hope of winning. The Gaze brothers had long moved on from those days, but there were still plenty more games to be played.

NO ROMAN HOLIDAY

The joy and satisfaction that comes with being named in your first Olympic Games team is one to be savoured. After all, there is no such thing as being a former Olympian. Once you are an Olympian, you are an Olympian forever. Yet the sweet sensation of being picked for the Australian team to go the 1960 Olympics also provided another sobering insight to the harshness of sport and how to deal with certain situations.

The 1960 Olympic team was chosen during the 1959 Australian Championship in Adelaide and announced immediately after the final game with every player in attendance. It was great if you were named in the team, but terrible if you missed out after thinking you had a real chance of making it. It put players in a terrible situation, and I vowed never to do that if I ever became coach of Australia. Six South Australians were named in the team, with three players from New South Wales, only two from Victoria – Bill Wyatt and me – and one from Western Australia, the latter a surprising choice given the selectors believed it might help promote the game in Perth.

Between 1956 and 1960, there was no international competition, unless you count a handful of games against teams from visiting US Navy ships when they docked at Port Melbourne and elsewhere. So, with six players and the coach, Erik Erkins, from Adelaide, it was decided the team would convene in the SA capital for an extended preparation, training several times a week and playing in the local competition. It was a sound plan with good support from the SA association and their clubs, and with accommodation supplied and jobs organised. While neither of us had any qualifications, Bill and I were given jobs as painters in a new suburb called Elizabeth, north of Adelaide. But by the time we travelled to Elizabeth, took time for lunch and then left early to get back for training, our paintbrushes were rarely dipped in a tin.

We were housed together, hosted by Dick Hughes, who was also on the team, and his wife Anne. They were a great couple and Anne always went out of her way to do whatever was needed for her guests. Unfortunately, her ability in the kitchen didn't always match her enthusiasm. One night as we sat down to dinner, I sniffed the cabbage on my plate and offered a quizzical look to the others. Anne asked if there was anything wrong, but nobody was game to comment. So, Anne went and checked the pot used to boil the cabbage, discovering a bar of soap was the reason for some extra froth and flavour. After that, Bill and I made sure we had a stash of emergency rations, just in case.

The progress of the house Bill and I were painting was in keeping with the progress of the team. We never quite got the job finished before heading to Rome, and neither did the team. The results of our games in the SA league were to be expected, but our winning margins gradually decreased and so did our motivation. There was no offensive structure to speak of and the reality was the team, which was harmonious from start to finish, was no better prepared as we readied to leave for the Games than when we had arrived in Adelaide.

Nor was there any improvement in travel plans as we departed for Rome on what can only be described as a milk run. With the pre-Olympic qualifying tournament in Bologna due to start on August 13, we left Adelaide on July 30 and made two stops before we even left Australia.

The first stop was Alice Springs, where we played two games on the outdoor courts, and the second was in Darwin, playing three more games scheduled around a civic reception and coaching clinics for juniors and seniors. The accommodation in Darwin was good, complete with mosquito nets and a warning that more than three bites would require a blood transfusion.

The next stop was Manila and the eye-opening sight of the city's depressing slums, crammed with rickety huts in danger of being swept away if the river broke its banks. Not two blocks away, the team was staying in one of the city's best hotels. Each room had the luxury items of telephone, air conditioning, radio, shower and toilet. The geckos running up and down the wall were easy to live with while they kept down the fly and mosquito population. But one training session in the oppressive heat and humidity let us know we would be in trouble in the two games scheduled against the Philippines.

There were 12,000 people inside the Rizal Memorial Stadium – 2,000 of them in courtside seating and the rest ominously behind wire mesh stretching from floor to ceiling. Australia scored the first basket of the game and that was our only lead of the game as the Filipinos ran us off the court, turning a 12-point halftime lead into a 27-point win. The newspaper report after the game suggested it would take Australia 15 years to catch up to the Philippines. Somehow, just 24 hours later, we lost by three – 82-79 – amid apologies from the home players about the refereeing, knowing full well they were likely influenced by gamblers with money on the game. The same sports journalist wrote after the game, 'Maybe it won't take 15 years for Australia to catch up'.

Basketball in the Philippines is a religion. It is also corrupt given the amount of money that changes hands in betting on games and this quick stop was a small taste of what was to come years later. On a tour with Melbourne Tigers, we had three games scheduled against the country's three best teams. We won the opening game by 30 points and the second by a similar margin. We were happy, but others were not. When I asked one of the local administrators if he was happy with our team's performances, he expressed his disappointment. The first game, he said, had spoilt the betting angle and the fans immediately lost interest.

In another game, things got heated after one of the Filipino players had constantly niggled one of our players. After smiling and patting the local player on the head, things only got worse for our player as tensions continued to escalate until the referees intervened and calmed the situation. After the game we learned there had been no interest in betting on the outcome of the game. But, knowing we would win the game, a betting market had been created around the possibility of an all-in brawl; if an Australian or Filipino would be ejected; and all sorts of options. Whatever the betting outcome was, the game got to the finish without any more violence.

One disconcerting aspect on that first trip to Manila was the use of a pistol to signal the end of each half. Rather than a buzzer or horn, the timekeeper would fire a revolver loaded with a blank. It certainly got everyone's attention, especially the new kids in town. As did a sign at one of the many bars dotted around the city. The sign read: 'No guns or offensive weapons allowed on the premises'. I assume the timekeeper had to leave his gun at home.

Eventually we made it to Bologna for the pre-Olympic tournament, where the results were disappointing, but not surprising. Five teams from 18 were to advance to Rome for the Olympic tournament and Australia was up against it. Among the teams in Bologna were Yugoslavia, Czechoslovakia, Spain, Canada, Germany, Hungary, Poland and Greece. We finished bottom of Group D with an 0-4 record after losses to Poland, Israel, Greece and Switzerland, but beat Sudan and Great Britain in the classification games. We headed to Rome for the Games as spectators and then home to Australia with some lessons learned ahead of our next Olympic shot at Tokyo in four years.

FROM TOKYO TO MEXICO

Every couple of weeks, it seemed, Ken Watson would stick his head through my office door to tell me he was on the trail of a gun European player who had just arrived in Australia. More often than not, they turned out to be volleyball players or just rumours. But one time Ken was on the money was when he heard about Les and John Hody. The brothers were among the 200,000 people who had fled Hungary after the 1956 anti-communism uprising. A brutal invasion of Soviet troops crushed the uprising, killing at least 3,000 civilians and leaving 35,000 jailed or interned. It turned out the Hodys were the real deal as basketball players and we made a move to sign them for Church, the club that eventually became Melbourne Tigers. Alas, as was often the case then and well into the future, we were outmanoeuvred.

The grapevine was well and truly buzzing in Adelaide about the Hody brothers, and the City of Churches had a strong Hungarian basketball community. Before we knew it, a guy from Adelaide had driven to Melbourne and swooped up Les and John, who had anglicised their given names Laszlo and Janos. They were playing over in South Australia before we could even ask what size jersey they wore. Eventually, we did get Les and John a few years later. An excellent businessman, John knew there was more opportunity to make his fortune in Melbourne than Adelaide, so he moved east and his brother eventually followed. Having created a business in fashion knitwear, John was an absolute workaholic. He might have been up all night doing deals and his eyes were hanging out of his head, but he never missed a beat at training or in games.

Despite John's incredible work ethic on and off the court, Les was the better player and represented Hungary at several major events. After playing at the 1952 Olympics as a 17-year-old, Les won silver and gold medals at European championships and was made a legend of Hungary's Basketball Hall of Fame in 2012. But in 1964, Les was to be a key player for Australia at Tokyo, where he would become the first man to play Olympic basketball for two countries.

After the disappointment of the 1960 Olympics, Australia was due to play at the 1962 world championship in the Philippines. But the event was cancelled by FIBA, basketball's world governing body, and relocated to Brazil in 1963 after the Philippines Government refused to issue visas for the Yugoslavian team. Despite that, the Philippines still went ahead with a serious international tournament. While Australia, with John Hody in the line-up and Keith Miller replacing Eric Erkins as coach, did not win a game at that tournament, we were competitive. Except for the United States, we got within six points of every team during the last few minutes but could not finish the job. Despite the losses, we did gain a lot from the experience.

For the 1962 trip to the Philippines, Keith Miller decided the team would run the Melbourne Church offence, and it worked well considering we had little preparation and we were still novices on the big international stage. When we went to Japan for the 1964 pre-Olympic qualifier and subsequent Olympic tournament, Keith decided we would use *his* offence, which was basically a passing game with no structure and no rules. I had become Keith's de facto assistant coach and often took things into my own hands, calling the players together pregame to discuss our tactics and how we would approach things. It was not an ideal situation, but the team was compatible and competitive, and we had an excellent Olympic campaign.

Aside from a new coach, there were nine players at their first Olympics with only me, Bill Wyatt and John Heard remaining from the 1960 Games. Among the new players were migrants Mike Dancis and Les Hody; Michael Ah Matt, an exciting Indigenous player; Ken Cole, who was on the cusp of a long and controversial basketball career; and Werner Linde, perhaps the best pure shooter Australia has ever had. But none of them had the rapid and unlikely rise to the Olympic level as Brendon Hackwill.

As he did throughout his coaching days, Ken Watson would recruit players, especially juniors, by advertising, even if it was just by posting a small sign in a shop window. This time, Ken ran an ad in a newspaper that simply said: 'Big kids welcome to play basketball. Must be under 18 and tall'. Despite being older than 18, Brendon and his mate Mike Quinn responded to the ad and Ken found a spot for them in the senior Church program. After starting with the Church seconds, *Hack* progressed quickly and moved onto the bench for the first team, played well and was picked for Victoria. Taking his chance when a few players were injured, *Hack* was chosen for the 1964 Olympic team just 18 months after answering Ken's newspaper ad.

Used as a back-up big man in Tokyo, *Hack* played well, especially when he was in the game with his Melbourne teammates:

me, Bill and Les. But no sooner had *Hack* made it to the Olympics than he was gone again, this time to play football in the Victorian Football League with Fitzroy. At 193cm (6'4") *Hack* represented a giant in Australian football terms in the mid-1960s, and he managed 17 games for the *Lions* through 1965 and 1966. But it was a poor period for the club, and he enjoyed just one win with the firsts. Ken Watson was a Fitzroy supporter, which was no surprise as its ground was only 100 metres from his home. After watching *Hack* play, Ken dubbed him *The Ambulance* because *Hack* always seemed to arrive on the scene after the action had taken place. At least *Hack* could say he was part of one of Australia's best-ever Olympic campaigns, which might sound odd given we finished ninth of 16 in Tokyo.

Despite some misgivings among the players about the coach, Keith Miller was a good man and a wonderful servant to basketball, especially in Adelaide, where he was held in the highest esteem. Such was Keith's nature, he recognised the team was playing well and, while some of the players did not agree with or enjoy his method of substituting according to the clock, he did not mess with a good thing. There was the odd run-in, especially between Keith and Bill Wyatt, but the team stayed on an even keel and the results were excellent.

At the pre-Olympic tournament in Yokohama, we qualified for Tokyo with an 8-1 record, beating Canada, South Korea, Malaysia, Taiwan, Philippines, Cuba, Indonesia and Thailand. The only loss was to Mexico. It was a gruelling schedule with nine games in 10 days, and it prepared us for the Olympics, where we opened against the United States. The US was coached by Hank Iba and featured Bill Bradley, Walt Hazard, Mel Counts, Larry Brown and Jim Barnes, who had been taken by the New York Knicks with the first pick of that year's National Basketball Association draft. We lost 78-45 to the US and my abiding memory of that game is running into a screen set by Barnes, nicknamed *Bad News*. It sent a shudder through my entire body and I made sure to let Mike Dancis know he should tell me the next time the truck wearing No.4 was bearing down on me.

We bounced back to beat Peru, and South Korea. But in between we blew a chance to score what would have been a win of major significance. Silver medallist at the 1963 world championship, Yugoslavia shaped as a daunting opponent, to say the least. With our strategy of constantly changing defences to keep Yugoslavia off balance, there was only one point in it at half-time. Despite foul trouble, we hung in there in the second half and actually led by two with 10 seconds left and two free-throws to come. I watched from the defensive end of the floor as Scott Davie missed both free-throws and Yugoslavia controlled the ball after it was tipped back from the rim. In the blink of an eye, I was facing a two-on-one fast break and feeling very lonely. The Yugoslavia captain, Ivo Daneu, drove straight at me and through me. All I could see from my prone position on the court was the tying basket after Daneu passed to a teammate. We lost by four in overtime, but it was hard to take any satisfaction from the result.

Wins in the last two games of the tournament, including one over Japan in the playoff for ninth and 10th, left us at 4-5 and gaining plaudits for a major breakthrough on the international stage by an Australian team. What was worth considering above the simple win-loss record was that our four wins came at an average margin of about 11 points, and our four losses, aside from the 33-point defeat to the US, were by an average of fewer than five. We lost by four in overtime to Yugoslavia, by two to Finland, by one to Uruguay and by 12 to Brazil.

We closed with wins over Mexico and Japan, which were satisfying for at least two reasons. Beating Japan meant we defeated the host nation, and beating Mexico reversed the result from the qualifying tournament. In fact, that loss to Mexico in Yokohama set up the win in Tokyo. Before we played Mexico in Tokyo, I gathered the team together and, after what I had seen in the qualifying tournament, told them to play a 1-3-1 zone defence. It worked well and when Keith Miller suggested we might change our defensive strategy in the second half, I strongly suggested otherwise. We stayed in the 1-3-1 and won by 12.

In reality we were one or two baskets away from qualifying for the medal rounds at Tokyo and we had certainly done ourselves and Australian basketball proud.

As always at an Olympics, the opportunities presented off the court can be more lasting and more enriching than those on it. Aside from the American assistant coach of Japan, who thought I was trying to con him to get some intelligence ahead of our playoff, there were some friendships created and experiences shared. Among the people I connected with were US trio Hank Iba, the legendary coach; Larry Brown, who went on to become a Hall of Fame coach; and Bill Bradley, who won two NBA titles with the New York Knicks and then served the US Senate for 18 years before launching an unsuccessful presidential campaign.

During the Games, Bradley, a Princeton graduate and Rhodes Scholar, asked me if I knew any of the Soviet players well enough to organise a meeting with him. This was right in the middle of the Cold War, and events such as the building of the Berlin Wall and the Cuban Missile Crisis were still fresh and wary talking points. With Mike Dancis engaging his Latvian connections in the USSR team, he, Bill Wyatt and I dined with and observed some interesting conversation between the gold medal-winning future US senator and Soviet players Janis Krumins and Juris Kalnins.

When overseas, Bill Wyatt and I always made sure to take in as much as possible of the city we were visiting, and Tokyo was fascinating. The level of cooperation and trust among the citizens was amazing, which no doubt played its role in Bill, Mike Dancis and I seeing Dawn Fraser create Olympic history with a third gold medal in the women's 100m freestyle. None of us had tickets for the swimming pool, but the advice I had received four years earlier in Rome came in handy. With the pool adjacent to the village, it was perfect for a successful raid. I told Mike and Bill to put on their Australian tracksuits, wet their hair and drape a towel around their necks. As we approached the entrance, we broke into a fast walk, flashed out accreditation passes at the security guard before he had a chance to even to glance at them, and then scattered. Our impersonation of Olympic swimmers was a success and we were there to see Dawn Fraser win another gold medal, the last major act of her Olympic swimming career, banned after accusations she stole a flag from the Emperor's Palace.

Just before the Mexico City Olympics of 1968, swimming officialdom lifted Fraser's ban, but she had no time to prepare and qualify for a bid at a fourth straight gold medal, so she stayed home. In some ways, the Australian basketball team suffered a similar fate, although we did get to Mexico. Unfortunately, we didn't make it out of the pre-Olympic qualifying tournament. Four years after a brilliant showing in Tokyo, we went 0-4 at Monterrey and suffered the embarrassment of a loss to Indonesia.

Despite the breakthrough performance at the 1964 Olympics, it was a case of one step forward and two steps – maybe three – backwards for the Australian team. The men running the Australian Basketball Federation (later known as Basketball Australia) decided they could not afford to send the team to Uruguay for the 1967 world championship, so there was no serious preparation in terms of international competition. A handful of games against a couple of US colleges, the New South Wales state team and a second-string Australian line-up only served to show we needed more work during our two weeks together before departure for Mexico.

Appointed Australia coach for a second stint, Ken Watson invited Stu Inman to help with our pre-Olympic preparation, bringing in a fresh set of eyes with extraordinary basketball knowledge. A player at San Jose State after World War II, Inman was good enough to be drafted into the still-fledgling NBA. But he opted to go straight into coaching at high school level, eventually returning to San Jose State as head coach before a long career as an NBA scout and general manager, most notably with the Portland Trail Blazers. Even with Stu's help we knew we needed plenty of luck before we could even think about getting to Mexico City.

There were five Victorian players – all from Melbourne Church – in the team for 1968, and Ken was the coach, so we should have had the basis of a strong outfit. But one player not in the team was Bill Wyatt, and I knew we would miss him greatly. An automatic selection, Bill had to make himself unavailable after the death of his father left him running the family business and no time to commit to an Olympic Games campaign. Even so, our arrival in Mexico coincided with some good news and some bad news. The good news was the confidence and cohesion of the group suddenly came together. The bad news was nobody escaped a rapid and random bout of *Montezuma's Revenge*. We were making fast breaks for the toilet at a regular rate. While I was not hit as hard as others, I still lost six kilograms over three weeks and was looking gaunt by the time we left for home.

After an all-night train trip from Mexico City to Monterrey, the welcome from local officials and a mariachi band might have been the highlight of our pre-Olympic tournament. It featured plenty of incompetence from score bench officials and referees and, not to shift blame for the results, the Australian players as we went 0-4 and left town with our heads down. Centre Carl Rodwell was fouled out twice when he only had four fouls, a crucial factor in the four-point loss to Poland. We also never came to grips with the really poor refereeing in the loss to Spain, keeping it close before losing by 19, and we could not get over the line in a close one against Uruguay, going down by two.

But the greatest disappointment of the pre-Olympic tournament was purely and simply down to the team, beaten by Indonesia in the second game, when we still had a chance to qualify. While it took Ken some time to find an effective on-court combination against Indonesia, we shot poorly and never looked like winning.

After a three-way tie, Spain and Poland advanced to the Olympic tournament ahead of Uruguay, and Australia finished bottom of the group. It was disappointing, but important to keep in context that Australia was still an emerging basketball nation and a couple of baskets – and a couple of referees' calls – either way can make a huge difference to the overall outcome.

After the disappointment of Monterrey, we regrouped to win a minor four-team tournament in Guadalajara. It was not a particularly momentous event, and nor was the bullfight we attended. The feature was to be a famously retired matador applying the finishing touches to a bull already so wounded it was hideously cruel. Some of the locals were as unimpressed as I was, leaving the arena never wanting to see another bullfight ever again.

On the contrary, the return to Mexico City provided an opportunity to witness some outstanding Olympic moments, including the US winning gold over Yugoslavia and the remarkable Kresimir Cosic. A 211cm guard, Cosic was the prototype of the modern Europe basketballer and on his way to becoming one of the world's all-time greats. There was also Bob Beamon's miraculous long jump world record, but two memorable moments for Australians were surrounded by much greater gravitas. Running in the thin air at altitude, Ron Clarke collapsed trying to win the 10,000 metres, prompting fears for his life, while sprinter Peter Norman became a part of civil rights history and folklore. After winning a silver medal in the 200 metres, Norman wore a badge that read *Olympic Project for Human Rights* and stood on the victory dais with Tommie Smith and John Carlos as they delivered a *Black Power* salute to protest the oppression of black Americans.

It was the last time Peter Norman would race at an Olympic Games. I had also played basketball for the final time at an Olympic Games and Ken Watson had coached his last game. By the time of the 1972 Olympic Games in Munich major changes had been made.

A DOT IN HISTORY

In terms of modern world history, Sarajevo holds a major significance. The shot that led to the eventual outbreak of World War I was fired in Sarajevo with the assassination of Archduke Franz Ferdinand. Over the past 600 years, Sarajevo has fallen under the rule of the Ottoman Empire; the Austro-Hungarian Empire; the State and Kingdom of Slovenes, Croats and Serbs; and the Kingdom of Yugoslavia (later Socialist Federal Republic of Yugoslavia) before finally gaining independence as Bosnia and Herzegovina. The city has also been involved in many wars and conflicts, most recently as Bosnia declared its independence from Yugoslavia in 1992.

So the 1970 world championship, hosted by five Yugoslav cities including Sarajevo, is a mere dot in the history of the region. It could be argued the performance of the Australian team at those world titles also registered a mere dot with a campaign that encapsulated all of the bad and some of the good that had come to be associated with our national team. In historical terms, it was the first time Australia had attended an official men's world championship. It was the intention to compete in Uruguay in 1967, but those in charge of the Australian Basketball Federation decided they could not afford it.

The selection of coach and team, as always, provided the first talking points as we prepared for Yugoslavia. After the job of Olympic coach had gone from Ken Watson to Erik Erkins to Keith Miller to Ken Watson, it was decided John Raschke would be the man in charge of the 1970 campaign. While John had a lot of basketball experience, hindsight showed he may not have been ready, or equipped, to coach the national team.

As for selection talking points, I was one of them, especially in my own mind. So, it was a surprise when I was named in the Australian team for the world championship. At 33, I was an old hand and considered by some to be past my prime. It was a delight and an honour to be in the first Australian men's team to contest a world championship, following the women, who had done so in 1967. Only five players returned from the 1968 Olympic team: me, Ray Tomlinson, Ken Cole, John Gardiner and Albert Leslie. The seven new players were Huba Nagy, Teddy Graham, Dennis Kibble, Russell Riches, Russell Simon, Brian Kerle and Richard Duke, which provided an interesting mix of personalities, inexperience, and youthful exuberance.

As always for any Australian basketball team, a trip to Europe provided plenty of travelling, and it did not always go smoothly. As an example – and it might have been this trip or another earlier tour – the challenges sometimes started even before boarding the aircraft to leave Australia. Sitting at the terminal in Melbourne waiting to board our flight to Sydney for the international connection, it dawned on me that the delay seemed out of the ordinary. I approached the desk and asked about our flight and when we would be boarding. The attendant told me the flight had already gone. The only member of the travelling party on the plane was the team manager, the man responsible for ensuring nobody missed the flight. Fortunately, we hastily arranged another flight, caught up with our team manager and got the connection.

For this journey to Yugoslavia, we used a variety of transport, going via Manila, Chinese Taipei, Hong Kong, Zurich, Madrid and Bologna, finally arriving in Sarajevo.

We played three games in Manila, with John Raschke using a different starting line-up in each one. We also took in some local entertainment at different ends of the spectrum: one being at a venue down a few alleyways that was best described as a live demonstration of the *Karma Sutra*; the other being with a few thousand locals for jai alai, the fast-paced sport that drew big television audiences and plenty of betting.

From the heat and humidity of Asia, we landed into the cold of Europe and a stopover in Zurich. We had no games organised, and not even a court booked for a training session, so some of us took a train to Luzern and a cable-car up a mountain. The scenery was spectacular, but only the driving snow might have been stronger than the intestinal fortitude of those on the cable-car, given it was quite a shaky journey up and down the mountain. With such a sight-seeing feel to the stop in Switzerland, Huba Nagy made the most of it, using his camera to perhaps set a world record for taking photos of beautiful young Swiss women. His ability to get the ladies to pose for him could only be admired, but I have always wondered if Huba even had any film loaded.

The next stop in Italy was for a game against Virtus Bologna, losing to the club team led by American Terry Driscoll, and then we headed to Madrid for a tournament and the most important games of our preparation. After being tied with Spain at half-time, we lost by 10 as Cliff Luyk and Wayne Brabender – two Americans who had become Spanish citizens and key players for the dominant Real Madrid team of that era – led the way. We also got smashed by Brazil, trailing by as much as 30 during an embarrassing first half. Our lack of size against the bigger and more athletic Brazilians was telling, and the cracks were already starting to show on and off the court.

While all the players got on well and there was a good sense of camaraderie, the lack of playing time for those at the end of the bench did start to take its toll on them. Which is fully understandable. When they did get the chance to play, it was for minimal time. For Russ Riches, the situation was exacerbated by foul trouble, while Teddy Graham ran into trouble as the referees continually called him for carrying the ball, a move he had been able to get away with playing in Melbourne. But there was no question the greatest amount of tension was being generated by the coach. There was ill-ease between John Raschke and team manager Bill Feltham, prompted by John's outburst at Bill about dinner arrangements in Bologna. Then John absolutely lost it at half-time of the Brazil loss in Madrid. During his rant, John accused us of being weak and careless, setting quite a pace with a string of expletives, some I had never heard before. As such, his call to play harder, run faster and look after the ball lacked any detailed instruction or change of tactics, and the second half was spent basically keeping the margin where it was.

So that was how we arrived in Sarajevo for our three group games against Czechoslovakia, the United States and Cuba. Having played Slavia Prague in a series of games in Australia, we knew what to expect and felt good about being able to take the game to the Czechs. In a departure from his normal approach,

Doc Raschke asked for input and suggestions from the players ahead of the Czechoslovakia game. Ken Cole and I agreed the key was to apply pressure to limit the influence of the Czech big men, Jiri Zidek and Jiri Konopasek. We started big, went small and tried everything in between, but lost by 24. A 37-point loss to the United States followed and we closed Group A with a defeat to Cuba, sending us to the classification round in Skopje.

After a win over United Arab Republic, we lost four straight to Panama, Cuba, Canada and South Korea. The abiding on-court memories were of Panama duo Davis Peralta and Pedro Rivas, two great scorers who gave us migraines more than headaches, and of South Korean forward Shin Dong-Pa, who was one of the best and purest shooters I have ever seen. Using non-stop motion, running off multiple screens, Shin was the 1970 version of Steph Curry and led the world championship in scoring with a touch under 33 points per game.

The abiding off-court memories of Skopje were of boredom and the accommodation, both of which were put down to the effects of the environment. With constant rain during our time in Skopje, we were basically confined to barracks outside of games and shoot-arounds, and Ray Tomlinson and I became amateur entomologists studying the ants that trekked back and forward between our huts and their nests. There was also a lack of running water in our huts, which, aside from the obvious need to shower elsewhere, made for a rancid smell after the accumulation of waste in what was supposed to be a sewage system.

The accommodation manager explained the lack of running water quite simply: the huts were on a hill and it was difficult for the water to flow uphill. The lack of water was also blamed on an earthquake that occurred in 1964, as was the lack of mail being delivered to the team. On investigation, the mail had been delivered to Sarajevo's best hotel. The postman simply assumed we would be staying there, even though the addresses on the letters said otherwise. The mail also prompted a tense show-down between Australian teammates, one winding up the other about the suspected contents of a letter from a female admirer. Fortunately, the threat of physical violence did not ensue.

With our tournament over, we headed to Ljubljana in the north-west of Yugoslavia, a region that is now Slovenia, to watch the final stages of the event. It was a double-edged opportunity for me: trying to meet as many officials and coaches from the US, Russia and Yugoslavia in a bid to organise tours to Australia; and to watch the world's best players fight for the medals. The responses about tours and visits were relatively positive, and Yugoslavia won the gold medal, led by captain Ivo Daneu, the man who mowed me down at Tokyo in 1964. Brazil took silver behind Wlamir Marques, my idol since seeing him play at the 1956 Olympics and, in 1991, named one of FIBA's greatest 50 players.

While veterans Daneu and Marques stood out, there was one other player I was keen to get a look at. Contrary to the Olympics, the United States did not always name its strongest teams for the world championship. That was the case in 1970 as the US fin-ished fifth. On the roster was a 17-year-old who had just finished high school. The talk about Bill Walton had built up my expec-tations of the teenaged centre, but I was far from impressed with the few minutes he was given towards the end of games. While

Walton was tall and athletic, and it was a special achievement to have been named on the team, I was sure there were hundreds just like him back in the US. A year or two later during a US tour, I saw Bill Walton playing for UCLA and he had gone from a kid at the end of the American bench to a dominant college superstar. Beset by injuries during his career, Walton won two NBA titles with Portland and Boston and was named the 1978 NBA MVP. It was, in some ways, a lesson learned – or a reminder – that potential comes before prosperity.

On reflection, I felt privileged to be part of the Australian team at the 1970 world championship. I was probably the last player picked for the team and had no greater expectation than coming off the bench in a back-up role. But that changed and I was pleased to start, play more minutes and have a more significant impact on the team. The results were disappointing, and I felt we could have done better with more structure on offence and defence. But I also concede John Raschke had a tough job of trying to pull a team together and implement any kind of plan with such a limited preparation.

The 1970 world championship was my last appearance at a major event as a player for Australia. Soon enough I would be fully aware of – and experience – the trials, tribulations, obstacles and criticism that Doc Raschke endured. But the dot in history that was the world championship would provide something much bigger for me and for Australian basketball.

WHISTLE BLOWERS

I'm somewhat proud that during my playing career I received only two technical fouls. One was for simulating counting. We were lined up for the opposition to shoot two free-throws. On a previous trip to the foul line, the shooter took forever to get his shot up. The rule is to shoot within five seconds. I started moving my hand to count the seconds elapsing. It might not have been too subtle, and the referee did not enjoy it. Beep! Technical foul! I wouldn't have thought it was a severe offence. The second technical foul was for inappropriate language. I said 'shit'. Beep! Technical foul!

As a coach there were a few more technical fouls committed and called. But the tech I remember most vividly was one I certainly did not deserve. It was during a National Basketball League game. Usually I would let my assistant coach Al Westover offer the loud objections to the referees and then I would have a quiet word to the officials. It was something of a good cop-bad cop thing. The arrangement was working during this particular game until we reached the limit. During a break in play, one of the referees, Billy Mildenhall, came over and said, 'That's enough. Anymore and you'll get a technical'. I said, 'Fair enough'. Beep! Technical foul!

After the game, Billy approached me and asked what I had said when he whistled the technical foul. I told him, 'Fair enough'. Billy replied, 'That's what I thought you said, but at the time I thought it was something else'. So, he knew he had made a mistake and was big enough to ask about it and admit it. Which is why Billy Mildenhall was one of the NBL's and Australia's best and longest-serving referees along with men like Eddie Crouch and Ray Hunt, and before and early in their careers, John Holden.

Those few technical fouls were only a couple more than Dick Mason was called for on our bench, and he was a referee. An excellent official and broadcaster for the ABC, Dick was a guest on one of our US tours. Quite a verbose, colourful and forthright individual when required, Dick was living every pass and shot of our game against the University of Minnesota. When the refs missed a call late in the game, they did not appreciate Dick's opinion or how it was expressed. We were hit with a bench tech, Minnesota made the free-throws and we lost a close game.

A couple of men who made an important mark on the game as referees, especially during my playing days, were Les Dick and Sid Taylor. During the 1960s and early 1970s, Les and Sid were among our top referees. Nominated to referee at the 1970 world championship, Les was a stickler for the rules and would not back down to anyone when he was officiating. This became a problem for Les in Yugoslavia in 1970. The Europeans allowed for a looser interpretation of the travel rule, allowing an extra step at the end of a dribble in most cases. Not Les. He called the game by the book and this exasperated the European players and coaches, even the referees. After Les had called a travel, some of the European players would stop and make theatrical gestures towards him. But Les received no sympathy from anywhere or anyone, and it was disappointing he was not appointed to the medal games later in the tournament.

An excellent referee and referees' administrator, Sid provided some memorable comic relief at a meeting of the Australian Basketball Federation in the late 1960s without even being in the room. Among the topics on the agenda were Olympic Games reports, plans for the next world championship, the appointment of a national-team coach, and the proposed introduction of a national club competition. It is fair to say it was a serious meeting and, at times, tense. During the meeting, a staff member handed Bob Staunton a note, and Bob happily read the message for the meeting to hear. 'Bob, would you please check my room? I have left my false teeth behind. Thanks, Sid.' The gravity of appointing the Australian coach and preparing for a world championship quickly turned to levity, wondering where Sid's teeth were and how he had lost them in the first place.

Given the often-adversarial relationship between players, coaches and referees, I'm not sure if anyone has a favourite referee. But if I did have a favourite, it might have been Henry Perazzo, who was an excellent official and a tireless worker for improving and educating referees. During Henry's era, referees almost had to learn on the job, and he had a marvellous instinct for what was fair and what to call.

Indeed, Henry officiated at two Olympics – 1956 in Melbourne and 1960 in Rome. It was only after returning home from the 1960 Games that I heard about how popular Henry had been with the Italian fans. Given his Italian surname and his demonstrative style when making calls, Henry was loved in Rome. What capped it for the locals was Henry's signal for a hands foul, or what might have been referred to in those days as chopping or hacking. Henry's version of the signal was for his hand to come across his forearm, very much like the 'up yours' insult the Italians know so well. Any time Henry called a hands foul, the Italians were going crazy as Henry put on a show for them.

Being able to perform in the tense and sometimes frenzied atmosphere of the Olympic Games did not mean Henry was beyond being rattled, at least away from the court. During the early 1960s, Henry was one of several Victorian referees attending the Australian championship. Finances dictated that hotel rooms were shared, and Henry was bunking with another Melbourne ref. It is fair to say Henry's roommate was flamboyant and extroverted on the court but was a little more circumspect with his private life. Except for one night during the tournament. The next morning, Henry came up to me, all speechless and flustered. 'I came home last night,' Henry finally started, and X 'was in bed with another man'. It was an experience Henry never thought he would have encountered and a situation that was still rather taboo at the time. These days, Henry might not have even blinked.

There have been many relationships between and involving referees over the years, and not all of them have enjoyed a happy ending. Such as the referee from back in the old Albert Park days. Every night he was rostered on for games, he always asked to work on Courts 7 and 8 at the southern end of the stadium. As he headed out with his whistle, he would say, 'If anyone calls, I'm down on the back courts'. It turned out he wasn't always on the back courts. Sometimes he was over the back fence, enjoying an intimate rendezvous with a woman who was not his wife. Most of us were oblivious to this situation until the night his wife stormed into Albert Park and took to the unfaithful referee with a knife. The one time he did happen to be on the back courts turned out to be a painful time.

There was another long-standing ref at Albert Park I remember well, and we never had to worry about him slipping out the side door for some amorous activities. That was because he basically never moved from his spot on the floor. We nicknamed him *Sleepy* for his lack of movement, but he was incredibly reliable in terms of turning up to fulfil his shift. In fact, *Sleepy* refereed every night of the week, saving his pittance to put down a deposit on a house. He always asked to be rostered onto Court 6, which we did, and he would stand there with the game going on around him. *Sleepy* was a good guy, but possibly a little questionable with his officiating ability.

Refereeing and organising referees was, is and always will be a thankless task. So, we have much to be thankful for when referees do turn up and work a game. We probably have even much more to be grateful for when it comes to some of the pioneers of refereeing in Victoria. When I first started playing, the games were in church halls and army drill halls scattered around the city, and there was a band of referees who committed to being there whenever we were. It is cliché, but without those referees, there would not have been games and basketball could have been doomed in Victoria and Australia. They worked for peanuts, they loved the game and became part of the fabric and culture.

There were distinct personalities among the referees, too, depending on where you were playing. At the youth and Police Boys clubs, the refs had a harder edge and could look after things well if the action got too willing and physical. The referees who did the games at the various church associations were quieter in keeping with the environment.

My first games were at the Try Boys club in South Yarra. The court was about as big as a decent-sized kitchen and living area in a suburban house. It was so small you could shoot from the opposite free-throw line. That was probably a good thing for the refs, especially Jack Smith. Jack was rather large and never ran too hard. His lifetime reffing buddy was Wally Patterson, who was a little humpback. They were joined at the hip when it came to calling games. They were Like Laurel and Hardy – big and little – and always good for a laugh and story. One night they were doing a women's game at Albert Park and one of the players was having trouble making a shot. After another miss, the frustration got too much and she yelled at the ball, 'Get in you c&*^!'. To which her opponent smartly replied, 'If it was as big as yours it would go in easily'. Jack and Wally couldn't tell that story enough times in the referees' room that night.

The referees' room was an important hub for our game officials. They could gather to tell stories, discuss situations and feel a part of the game and the culture and their own brotherhood. The camaraderie of the referees was just as important as that of any player and coach because without the referees, basketball would be unable to continue in formal competition. We should be thankful for every referee who has pulled a whistle over his or her head, even those who felt a counting motion was worthy of a technical foul.

PART 3

The Coach

THE GEORGETOWN
PLAY

The essence of coaching – or the perception of coaching – was perhaps boiled down to a last-second play when Melbourne Tigers were on a tour of the United States. We had fought Georgetown University on every trip up and down the floor and now we had a chance to win the game with the final possession.

I called a timeout to draw up a play to get the last shot. It was our standard out-of-bounds play, which we had practiced almost every day. All I had to do was remind the players of their positions and our priority for taking what we hoped would be the winning shot. Andrew Gaze was to be the first priority and, if the defence had him covered, Paul Stanley was the next option. The teams went back on the floor and, seeing how we were positioned, the Georgetown coach, John Thompson, called a timeout to reset his defence. Which was a good thing because none of my players, except Nigel Purchase, who was designated to make the inbounds pass, were in the right spots to execute the play.

So, we drew the play again in the second timeout and returned to the floor. The ref handed the ball to Nigel to make the inbound pass and our four other players started moving and screening. As Andrew moved to catch the pass, Paul Stanley, instead of moving away from Andrew, moved toward him. Paul's defender bumped into Andrew's defender, leaving him open for the three-point shot we needed to seal the game and, at the same time, make me look like a genius coach.

It was also a shot that made history. This was the first time Georgetown had ever lost a preseason game on its home court. Even though it was not how the play was intended to work, it *did* work, and most people would have had no idea. Instead, they saw a coach draw up a play in a timeout and his team score the winning basket.

Coaching was something I have always done, even before I was doing it. By studying all the best players and teams and their methods at the 1956 Olympic Games, I was coaching myself to get better as a player. Soon enough, I was something of a de facto assistant coach while playing for Melbourne Church, Victoria and Australia. It wasn't, in many ways, a conscious move in those situations. Having coached junior club and state teams during the 1960s, the move to coaching at the elite level was more a natural evolution. Until Ken Watson stepped in and made it more of a revolution.

After Melbourne Church won another South Eastern Conference championship, Ken and I were finalising plans for a tour of the United States and Europe towards the end of 1970. While I was considering the schedule of games against Big Ten Conference college teams and some of Europe's best clubs, Ken was thinking something else: he wanted me to replace him as head coach. I rejected the proposal out of hand, believing I still had a couple of good years left as a player. I recalled Bill Russell being asked why he continued to log big minutes as player-coach of the Boston Celtics, and he replied, 'Because I'm the best player I've got'. I could not be that bold or presumptuous, but Ken was insistent and said I could play as much as I wanted during the tour and he would be there as assistant coach. It was a good chance to at least test the situation, so I agreed to become the new Melbourne Church head coach. I stayed in the role – it was never a job – for the next 35 years.

Little did I know then, and I still only suspect it, that Ken's move for me to become coach of Melbourne was tied to something a lot bigger – coaching the Australian national team. After the disappointment of the 1970 world championship under John Raschke, Ken knew the Australian Basketball Federation would be looking for a new coach. Ken also knew because of our failure to qualify for the 1968 Olympic tournament with him as coach, there was no chance he would get another shot with the national team. Beneath his fatherly exterior, Ken had some cunning and street smarts, and his plan was to use his influence as secretary of the ABF to steer me into the job as coach of Australia. Whatever the politics and machinations behind the scenes, that was how it panned out and I was named coach for the 1972 Olympics, going from peer to boss in a short space of time.

There are plenty of things I have witnessed and experienced during my time in basketball, but the most important thing I have learned is that you can never stop learning and you can never stop evolving. The day you become closed to listening to rational advice, adopting new methods, considering new strategies and techniques is the day you stop becoming a good coach. People will point at me now and say the Tigers ran the Shuffle offence for decades, so it's a bit contradictory to preach an open mind and evolution. What those people don't understand is that the framework of the Shuffle stayed the same, but with many, many subtle tweaks over the years to keep it constantly changing. Fans and media would see us operating the Shuffle and say, 'Well, Lindsay's running the same offence for the 600th year in a row'. We were, but they did not see the changes and options we had installed during the off-season.

During that first overseas tour as Melbourne coach, I resisted Ken's urgings to go into games off the bench. I felt as coach, I should coach. But I eventually did defer to Ken's insistence if I felt we needed a bit of help on the floor. One game I played was in Springfield, where Dr James Naismith invented basketball, and that was more out of wanting to be part of a historic occasion than anything else. But fate intervened to indicate coaching was now my role rather than playing, when I injured my knee in the very next game and was confined to the bench for all but the last few games on the European and Asian legs of the tour. We played quite well and, with club rivals Brian Kerle, Russell Simon and Robbie Johnstone as guest players, were competitive in almost every game. As much as the tour was about experience for the players, it was also about me gaining experience and knowledge as a coach, sometimes more so about what not to do.

We attended a tournament in Idaho and were invited to observe as one of the college coaches gave his pre-game talk. This should have been an opportunity to savour and we made sure to arrive early, sitting to the rear of the room and out of the way. The players filed in and sat at the front and stayed quiet until the coach arrived. Taking up his spot in front of the team, the coach solemnly asked one of his players if he had tied his shoelaces correctly. 'Yes, sir,' came the reply. The coach asked another player the same question. Same response. Then there was deathly silence for what seemed like one or two minutes. The tension was finally broken when the coach clapped his hands loudly and shouted, 'Let's go!' With that, the players stormed out the door and, having anticipated some words of tactical instruction, we were left dumbfounded and confused. That experience certainly underlined my basic thoughts of coaching: teach, instruct, and if you're going to say something, you'd better damn well having something worthwhile to say. That coach did neither.

The biggest driver for me as a coach was that I always wanted it to be a player's game. I could talk, instruct, teach, draw plays on the board, but the players are the ones on the floor having to make the plays, score the baskets and win the games. A coach is merely the conductor of the band, making sure things don't unravel from the tune we're playing. Simply put, most of the coach's work should be done before the game, not during it. If a coach prepares his team well enough, the input during games should be almost minimal: making substitutions, identifying mismatches and scoring opportunities, tweaking things to help the players and the team. The teaching and coaching at training should be about enabling the players to be in charge of their own destiny, knowing where to be and what to do in critical game situations without the coach needing to hold their hands and talk them through it.

The analogy I would give to support that philosophy is this: We're playing a grand final, there are five minutes left, I've used all my timeouts and there are thousands of screaming fans. There's nothing I can do yelling from the sidelines to make a difference. So, unless the players have been educated and trained to make their own decisions in those pressure circumstances, it's unlikely they're going to succeed. It's the preparation and having faith in the players that are the crucial elements. As the Georgetown game showed, calling a timeout for a last-shot play never guarantees anything.

If it was kept as a stat, I reckon I would have taken the least number of timeouts of any coach. If you call a timeout, you'd better have a reason for doing so. When you have only got two timeouts to use in the first half and three in the second (for much of my coaching career it was two and two) you cannot afford to waste them. Some coaches will use their timeouts for different reasons, and the main two reasons are probably to try to stop a scoring run by the opposition, or to set-up a play late in the shot clock or game clock. The trick is knowing when to use them and knowing even if you need to use them. Using a timeout to abuse or criticise someone for missing a shot or committing a dumb foul is a waste of time and energy and would likely have a negative effect. A timeout is only 60 seconds, so you need to be precise, get to the point of why you called the timeout and make sure the message is clear for the players to understand. If you're going to rant and rave, it's a wasted timeout. If you have got nothing to say that will help the team, don't call the timeout in the first place.

When the National Basketball League allowed television microphones to come into timeout huddles, I was vehemently opposed to it and would stay quiet until they had left. My point was I could not do my job properly – as I wanted to – with the microphones eavesdropping and the world listening. If I was critical of a player or used profanity – consciously or subconsciously

– while emphasising a point, I did not want that heard outside of the huddle. In my opinion, the microphones in the huddle add nothing to the telecast. My analogy is that a beautiful woman is still a beautiful woman when she is clothed. But take off her clothes and now all the mystery and intrigue are removed.

Cameras and microphones are now omnipresent in modern sport, not just basketball. While television helps pay the bills, microphones do not always do the coaches any favours. I remember watching an AFL game and the coach's pregame talk was broadcast. It was a major letdown. 'When we get the ball, run with it.' 'Help each other.' It was more like some kind of last-minute motivational speech rather than anything tactical or reminders of the game plan. It is the same in basketball, whether the NBL or NBA. 'Run harder.' 'Push through.' 'We need a rebound and a defensive stop.' Not really profound advice. It is the details that matter, and they must be the coach's priority. Remind the players about getting the correct angle on a cut, going shoulder-to-shoulder on a screen, how to play their defensive assignment. But we don't seem to see or hear that too often.

Some might accuse me of being an old, and old-fashioned, contrarian, but I didn't and don't always adhere to the populist or trending views on coaching and the game. For one thing, I disagree with the current move for Australia to develop its own unique style of game, implementing certain offensive structures or movements from juniors to seniors. The more variations we have, the more we learn about the game and how to attack various opponents and make adjustments. If we don't use and experience different methods, it is easy to become myopic and not get better.

When I say that, I don't mean on a team-by-team basis, but as an entire basketball community. Players, coaches and teams change so people get to experience various methods and strategies. If everyone uses the same approach, what's the point?

I was never too worried that other teams knew what the Tigers or the national team were doing with our offence. If teams tried to work us out and do something different, we learned from it and made adjustments. The opposition's efforts to counter us only made us better by looking at how we could approach certain scenarios differently and take advantage of teams who had not caught on to what others had. Even though the Tigers had been running the Shuffle since the 1960s, when Ken Watson brought it back from a visit to Auburn University, we never actually ran the exact same thing two years in a row. The principles of the offence were there, but so were many tweaks and different actions.

With the Shuffle, we could use it with the national team because the basic principles were easy to understand and execute. Then it was about making adjustments to suit the personnel and make sure we could play to our strengths. For instance, if we had Ian Davies and Steve Breheny on the team, as we did at the 1980 Olympics, we're not giving the ball to Steve for the majority of scoring opportunities. We're putting Ian in a role within the structure, so he gets the best looks and most opportunities because he was the better shooter and scorer. Whatever offensive structure a coach implements, it must be geared towards your best players and scorers, otherwise it's pointless. There is no use employing an equal-opportunity offence because it's not an equal-opportunity game. If you have a player who makes only 30 per cent of his field goal attempts, you are not going to give him 50 per cent of the team's shots, especially when you have one or two other players capable of hitting their shots at 50 per cent or better.

The modern game, especially in the National Basketball Association, appears to be little more than drive and kick-out a pass to an open man for a three-point shot, or using on-ball screening actions. It might be a simplistic outlook, but NBA offences have almost become one-dimensional. The three-point shot has become the dominant preference in the NBA and the trend is spreading. The statistical probabilities tell the coaches that X amount of threes is better than X amount of twos. That might be true, but X equals zero if the ball does not go in the basket. Which is why you need options within the offence. You can make your structure a laborious motion method or make it a sudden-death offence. Two passes can be just as good as 10, depending on the personnel and how the defence plays. But every team should have options.

Then again, you can have 1000 options in your offence, but none of them are worth a breath of air unless taught correctly or in the right manner.

The Tigers signed Americans Dave Simmons and Dave Colbert in the late 1980s. Both men were physical specimens and there was no question they could play basketball and would help our team in a big way. But during preseason training, they were struggling to grasp our offence. I started to get upset with them for their inability to learn the offence and said so. One of the Daves said, 'Lindsay, we've been doing this for six weeks and I've got no idea what we're doing'. The other Dave said, 'Neither do I'. At that moment, I received a coaching lesson of my own and realised I had been foolish. I had failed to recognise that even the most talented players still need to be taught and understand the basics. I had taken the lazy option, believing that because most members of the team were fluent in running the Shuffle, Dave and Dave would pick it up quickly without too many problems. The fault was with me, not them.

The next and most immediate step of the process was to ask whether we should adjust our method to suit the talent, or adjust the talent to suit the method? There is merit to both sides of the argument, but I decided to keep the method and work with Dave and Dave to understand it fully. So, I sent five who were fluent in the offence to one end of the floor and went to work with the two Daves and three other players. We went over every aspect of the offence laboriously and repetitively, starting with the most basic elements of screening and cutting. After a while, I was like Professor Henry Higgins in *My Fair Lady* when Eliza Doolittle masters her posh accent and he exclaimed, 'I think she's got it! I think she's got it! By George, she's got it! By George, she's got it!'. There should also be great credit to Dave and Dave for their persistence and willingness to learn, and they became valuable and key contributors to our team.

The other lesson from that situation is that it is never enough just to tell players what to do. So many coaches will say to players, 'I've told you over and over and over, don't do that'. But how many times has the coach explained and demonstrated what he wants done? That is the key to teaching. That is why you have training sessions. You can draw a play on the whiteboard and then walk through it on the court. You can demonstrate a skill. That's education and the player will more likely understand and be able to execute what the coach requires. In simple terms, you may TELL them what to do, but you must also SHOW them what to do.

Although I have my own definite views on the game and how it should be played and coached, I was always open to advice and was fortunate to have access to many brilliant basketball minds. Ken Watson was my first and most influential coaching mentor, and Stu Inman, who made his coaching bones at high school and San Jose State University before going to the NBA as a highly regarded scout and general manager, was another. Any time I needed advice, a sounding board or help, Ken and Stu were only a phone call away.

Even the briefest meetings could offer some learning, and some coaches left you with a brief insight that made so much sense. Such as the line from Lute Olson, who won a National Collegiate Athletic Association title with the University of Arizona. One of his favourite lines was: drive to score, not to explore. Translation: use your dribble effectively or pass the ball. Another coach, Bud Pressley, emphasised defence, while Paul Westhead had a love of just trying to outscore the opposition.

The legendary John Wooden, winner of 10 NCAA championships as head coach at UCLA, was a goldmine when it came to various philosophies such as team selection. The five factors when choosing a team, according to Wooden, are individual offence, team offence, individual defence, team defence and - the most important aspect - compatibility. Everyone can see how individuals fare on the court with the first four aspects, but only those on the inside know about a player's compatibility.

I followed that advice when picking the national team and compatibility was a factor. People would question why one player was chosen ahead of another, but I would never announce publicly that a player was omitted because of incompatibility, especially when it was because of his personality rather than basketball ability. That is why I have never publicly criticised any selections of the Australian teams for major events. We do not know what is happening on the inside regarding compatibility or team chemistry, but the coach will eventually be judged on the results.

One coach I respected for his achievements was Bob Knight, who made his name at Indiana University. But I did not necessarily agree with his methods. A winner of two NCAA titles, Knight's offence was predicated on a passing game, cutting and moving without rigid rules. He won plenty of games with it, but my view of it was that the lack of structure and rules reduced the likelihood of repeating a successful play. If you don't know how it happened because it came from an essentially freelance offence, how do you do it again exactly the same way? My theory is that structure allows you to read and take advantage of the defence and having the ability to adjust as the defence adjusts. It's about staying a step ahead of the opposition.

Perhaps it is worth mentioning Melbourne Tigers were Bob Knight's first opponents when he became coach of Indiana. I said in the post-game press conference, 'Our players got the same sense of satisfaction after making a successful pass as they normally got after making a successful shot'. That was due to the extremely intense defence Knight insisted his players apply, and I believe it was that level of defensive intensity, along with his famed motion offence, which led to his success.

A postscript to that game against Indiana was an invitation to supper at the home of Lou Watson, the coach who was moved aside for Bob Knight. Even though he was technically out of a job, Lou was still under contract to Indiana and still being paid his coaching salary. I asked Lou what his new job was at Indiana. Lou gave me a stunned look. 'I don't know,' Lou said. 'Hell, they can't fire me. I know too much.'

Apart from learning as much as I could during my coaching career, it was just as important to pass on that information and wisdom. So organising coaching courses and clinics became a staple in my role with the VBA. From that, we developed Level 0, 1, 2 and 3 courses and employed full-time coaching directors to get the game taught at schools and to ensure junior coaching was the best we could make it. It also helped coaches gain qualifications, so if clubs wanted to employ or recruit a coach, there was an easy reference about their level of basketball knowledge and education.

As a player and a coach, I devoured any basketball books, magazines or films that I could get my hands on. In the pre-Internet age, I would wait months for magazines or films to arrive in Australia, and they were so important to my development. In turn, I published my own coaching manuals. The first was *Beginning Basketball*, which is a self-explanatory title that covered the fundamentals of the game: the lay-up, jump shot, passing, dribbling. It was very basic but remains relevant today for novice coaches and players. The sequel was *Better Basketball*. That was more advanced and discussed defence and offensive structure and the various methods that could be used, such as the passing game, post action, Shuffle, high-low, and Triangle. In the vast global library of basketball reading, it was a speck of a contribution, but one that hopefully helped many players and coaches in Australia.

At the end of the day, that's what coaching is. It is helping others. Helping them improve as players, helping them understand the game, helping them to win games, helping them reach their potential and, when the relationships grow and develop over time, helping them as people away from the basketball court.

As with the last-second play against Georgetown, I could only help the players by drawing a play and talking them through the execution. It was up to them to do what was needed to be done on the floor, even if none of us could have possibly made two defenders collide to provide an open shot to win the game. That's the essence of coaching. You do as much as you can and then the rest is up to the players and the Basketball Gods.

OLYMPIC TERROR

Coming off back-to-back wins to close group play, things could only have been marginally better for the Australian men's basketball team at the 1972 Munich Olympic Games. It was disappointing to miss a spot in the knockout round by only one win, but we felt we had made strides as a team and within the international basketball community. Had Australia been able to flip either of the one-basket losses to Spain and Czechoslovakia, we would have been in the Olympic quarterfinals for the first time.

Next on the schedule was a game against host nation West Germany to start the crossover tournament for places nine to 12. Sitting in the dining hall of the athletes' village with a few players, that upcoming game might normally have been a topic of eager discussion and anticipation. Instead, it was totally irrelevant. 'This is surreal,' I said to my lunch companions. 'Here we are, able to have whatever we like in this luxurious dining hall with the best of everything. But just over the road there are people who don't know if they are going to be alive in the next hour.'

It was surreal and tragic and confusing. As we ate lunch, a group of Israeli Olympians had been taken hostage no more than 100 metres away, held by Palestinian terrorists from the Black September movement. By the time the darkest two days in Olympic history had finished, 11 Israelis and one West German police officer were dead. It wrapped a large sombre blanket over the Olympics, even as organisers seemed oblivious to the impact and magnitude of the tragedy. Such was the arrogance and/or ineptitude of those at the head of the International Olympic Committee, the Games continued throughout the hostage crisis, hoping to somehow maintain the Olympic ideals in the face of a dreadful tragedy.

The best part of any Olympic Games, aside from the actual competition, is life in and around the athletes' village. It might sound clichéd, but it is where the whole world comes together for two or three weeks to interact as peers, friends and sometimes more. There is a sense of youthful exuberance, fun and frivolity as athletes share meals, swap mementoes and phone numbers. Most athletes will remember fondly the vibe of the village during their Olympic experiences, forever blessed with dinner party conversation about some of the antics undertaken and the more sentimental moments.

Which was exactly how the 1972 Olympic Games had unfolded. The organisers wanted the Munich Olympics to be known as the *Carefree Games*. The 1936 Games in Berlin forever became known as the *Hitler Olympics*, a total parade of propaganda as the Nazis geared up their attempt to take over Europe, leading to World War II and some of the greatest atrocities known to man. The people overseeing the Munich Olympics hoped to create a new, friendly face of Germany to foreigners, still trying to shed the images of war-time aggressors.

As such, as the hosts tried to fulfil that image, it has been suggested security was relatively lax around Olympic venues and the athletes' village. In the dawn hours of September 5, 1972, eight terrorists wearing tracksuits took advantage of that light security, climbed a fence and broke onto the Israeli quarters. Two members of the Israeli contingent were killed almost immediately as they fought the intruders, allowing others to escape with their lives. The terrorists took another nine Israelis hostage: two weight-lifters, two wrestlers, three coaches, one referee and one judge. None would survive.

Incredibly, as the siege continued through the day and into the night, so did the Games. Aside from an obvious increase in security as police and military surrounded the Israeli compound, and a much quieter and more sombre atmosphere throughout the village, competition continued. There were many athletes opposed to the Games continuing and there was much confusion. The Australian basketball team was caught in that torn frame of mind and uncertainty given we were scheduled to play West Germany as the hostage drama continued to play out.

On reaching the stadium for the game, we were told Egypt had not arrived for its scheduled match against Philippines and there was doubt as to whether we would play West Germany. Without any indication of whether we were playing or not, the team started its on-court warm-up, only to be told the game was to be post-poned. FIBA secretary-general William Jones then declared the game would go ahead. We quickly tried to refocus and get loose, but it was a tough situation after such a dramatic and traumatic day.

The team was lethargic, lacked concentration and made plenty of errors against a West German outfit that had three sev-en-footers making it almost impossible to finish anywhere close to the basket. Down by 10 at half-time and as much as 14 in the second half, I gave the players one of the strangest instructions of my career. Given the German seven-footers were blocking everything around the basket, I told our team to not use the backboard for lay ups. I suggested we pull-up for a jump shot, or lay the ball in without using the backboard in a bid to negate the opposition big men, who were swatting the ball away every time we were about to convert an easy opportunity.

There were some dodgy calls as we fought back to take the lead, only to commit a turnover that started a German fast break and, likely, the winning basket. But a whistle sounded, a mystery foul came from nowhere, Ken James went to the free-throw line, made one of two with five seconds left and we held on to win, 70-69.

The win was a bright spot in a bleak couple of days and there was a stark reminder of what was unfolding at the village on our return. The streets around the athletes' village were barricaded, armoured cars patrolled ominously, helicopters circled in the sky and armed police and military were spaced at three-metre intervals around the perimeter. Our bus was diverted and when we finally got off, we were prevented from entering the village. Eventually, Australia's chef de mission Judy Patching was able to get us through with the help of a commandeered minivan. Life in our section of the village seemed almost normal, but the worst news was soon to filter through.

Helicopters flew the terrorists and hostages to a nearby airbase, where the Black September members would try to make their escape via a jet. A botched rescue/ambush attempt by German authorities ended with the remaining hostages killed, murdered as their kidnappers tried to evade capture. Organisers finally suspended all competition for 36 hours and a memorial service was held in the Olympic Stadium, attended by 80,000 people and more than 3000 athletes and officials. The remaining members of Israel's Olympic team went home and there was an undercurrent of feeling that, after such a tragedy, everyone else should have followed them. Yet the IOC refused to yield and was determined to uphold the Olympic ideals, declaring the Games must continue.

After three days off, Australia faced Poland in the playoff for ninth and 10th. We finished sixth in Group A, but had won three straight games, including the first crossover game against West Germany. So, a 91-83 win over Poland was a good finish to my first Olympic campaign as Australia coach after what had seemed a sometimes arduous and difficult build-up, trying to overcome the traditional issues with officialdom, logistics, selection and performance.

The selection of any national team usually brings some controversy, and it was no different for 1972. Except that we ran into controversy even before selectors Alan Dawe and Bob Elphinstone and I chose the team. It was suggested that former Americans who had recently become Australian citizens should be ineligible for selection. I disagreed strongly and reminded those involved that half of our 1956 Olympic team would have been barred under such a selection policy. I followed up with an ultimatum to the Australian Basketball Federation: if the team was not chosen on merit from all who were eligible, I was out. Once that issue was sorted out, it was essentially down to the players to choose themselves.

The selection process was innovative, if not revolutionary compared to previous Olympic campaigns, where the team was chosen on the basis of performances at the Australian Championship, usually with an unofficial quota system. But for Munich, we introduced training camps and used a tour of the United States, playing games against Big Ten Conference colleges, to see what the players could do under the pressure of top competition. Essentially, I wanted to get the squad together as often as possible so we could try to replicate a club situation, to get the players familiar with each other and to give them as many opportunities as possible to stake their claims for selection.

Aside from observation, we used volunteers to keep statistics at our Easter camp, charting as many drills as possible, including games of one-on-one, two-on-two and scrimmages. The combinations of the players were changed constantly, and patterns started to emerge with some players winning more often, regardless of who they were paired with. Conversely, there were players who lost more, and that provided some excellent insight and information to aid selection.

A major point of emphasis for the Easter camp was to gauge the quality and value of the big men on offer. We had Rocky Crosswhite, Brian Kerle, Ray Tomlinson and Peter Byrne as the big bodies set for a roster spot, so it came down to Tom Bender, Phil Lynch, Ric Longley and Graham Cuthbert basically fighting for one place. We went with Tom Bender in a team that was dominated by Victorians, much to the chagrin of South Australian fans with Werner Linde, Huba Nagy and Albert Leslie left at home. In the end, Glenn Marsland was the only South Australian on the 12-man team that was completed by Ken James, Ian Watson, Bill Wyatt, Eddie Palubinskas, Richard Duke and Toli Koltuniewicz.

With the team chosen, we picked up our first win of sorts when the players underwent fitness testing by the Australian Olympic Federation (later the Australian Olympic Committee) medical staff just before leaving for Europe. Eyebrows went up when Richard Duke outperformed one of the Olympic cyclists on the stationary bike and then casually recorded a 32-inch sergeant jump. Veteran Bill Wyatt was assessed to have a heart like a young bull, and seven-footer Tom Bender provided problems because there was a lack of equipment to suit his size. The best effort might have come from Toli Koltuniewicz, who got set for the ergometer test by asking what the best weightlifter had done. Told it was 145 pounds, Toli promptly squeezed the handles together for 150. Thinking there was an error, the examiner asked Toli to repeat the exercise. So he simply pushed out another 150-pound effort. It seemed we had at least chosen a fit and strong team.

On arrival in Munich, the famed German efficiency was a little lacking. With all the arenas and facilities close to the athletes' village, everything appeared good. Except we could only get a trickle of water out of the taps on the eighth floor, and it took five hours of shuffling between one enquiry desk to another to find out the location of the basketball training hall, and even longer to track down a training schedule. They were minor inconveniences and quickly forgotten once we got on the floor and got a few pre-tournament games in our legs. We smashed Great Britain by more than 50, beat the local Munich club team twice and then had a win over Senegal. The Senegal game included a complaint from the opposition coach that we were playing too hard for an exhibition game. On the contrary, I thought we were not playing with enough intensity.

We also beat Yugoslavia in a pre-tournament exhibition game, which led to an increased interest by Australian media. Although the game was described as an exhibition, there was plenty of edge. In fact, the increasingly competitive atmosphere created a tension that flared when Tom Bender got into a scuffle with his opponent and both were ejected. After that win, the Soviet Union coach asked if we would play them in a pre-Olympic game as well. I was polite and stalled a decision before saying our schedule was full.

There was also some feeling in the two games against Italy in the northern town of Varese. It was disappointing to find out the Italians had arranged for the games to be closed to the public, trying to protect their tactics and line-ups ahead of the Olympics. We played three periods of 30 minutes in the first game and played two halves of 35 minutes in the second. There were no official scores kept, but team manager Bob Staunton had us winning both games by narrow margins.

The Italians were led by Dino Meneghin, who stood 6'9", looked even bigger and was in the midst of a brilliant 28-year career at the top level. While there was a respectful nature about the preparation games, natural instinct kicked in a few times and the level of competition spiked, one time when Rocky Crosswhite tangled with Meneghin. Frustrated by the physical attention, Meneghin screamed into Rocky's face, 'Go home, mutha!'. Rocky turned away, making a gesture to indicate Meneghin's breath was on the rancid side. It gave everyone on the Australian bench a good laugh and a catchcry was born. Throughout the Olympics, even the hint of an altercation was enough to elicit a call of 'Go home, mutha!' complete with a heavy Italian accent.

Nine of the 12 players on the Australian team were Olympic rookies, but they did not lack confidence or preparation. Aware that many first-time Olympians suffer from fear of failure, I made sure to prepare each individual with knowledge of their role and what they could and should expect, hoping to lessen any nerves and anxiety.

After coming through the pre-Olympic qualifying tournament, Spain – still led by Cliff Luyk and Wayne Brabender – outlasted us to win by five in our first game. We should have won the game, but it did not help that all five Australian starters were sitting with me on the bench by the end of the contest, all fouled out. We led the United States after the opening 10 minutes of the next game before the Americans adopted a zone defence, dominated the rebound count and eventually posted a relatively easy victory. Following the game, US coach Hank Iba told the press, 'I didn't want to use a zone defence against Australia, as we wanted to save that for when we play Cuba. But the Australians were making it difficult for us with their offence, so we had to reveal our intentions'.

There was more foul trouble in a one-point loss to Czechoslovakia. We also hurt ourselves with missed free-throws down the stretch before a suspect out-of-bounds decision went the Czechs' way and led to the winning basket. A 16-point victory over Japan finally put a number in the Australian win column, but we could not match Cuba's athleticism in the next game, losing by 14. That loss ended our chances of making the quarterfinals, but it was also Australia's last loss of the Olympic tournament. We beat Brazil in a close game, despite the fact we were up at 5.30am for a 9am tip-off, giving us a departure from normal routine, and then we closed group play against Egypt. It had become clear that Eddie Palubinskas was our main scoring weapon, so Egypt employed a box-and-one defence in the next game, but it failed to totally slow down Eddie or Australia in an easy win.

The win over Brazil left a lasting impression on at least one person. Several years later, a Brazilian official approached me at a function. He said, 'Everyone hates playing Australia'. I was taken aback by the comment before he explained why, and I was then able to take it as a compliment. 'Munich, 9am,' he said, circling his finger to indicate our ever-moving offence and then chopping his hand on his arm to indicate our defence. He was saying the Australians always play hard and never give up. Similarly, a journalist was asked about the Australian style of play and he replied, 'They have the technique of the Americans, the aggression of the Europeans and the grace of the Asians'. Not bad. Another experienced basketball writer noted, 'They have a good army, but they need an air force'.

We closed the Olympics with wins over Germany and Poland to finish ninth with a 5-4 record and a belief we were on the right track. But before we left Munich, we got to witness probably the most controversial ending to a game in Olympic basketball history. Nor was it just any game. It was the gold medal game between the United States and the Soviet Union. The *Cold War* comes to a basketball court and it created another cold war that continues to this day.

In a low-scoring game, the Soviets led by one, but Doug Collins was on the free-throw line for the US after a hard foul sent him crashing to the floor. With unerring precision and repetition, Collins made both free throws to put the US up by one with three seconds left. The Soviets put the ball in play and failed to score as the US celebrated wildly. But one of the referees was blowing the pea out of his whistle, signalling that the USSR had called a time-out before the ball went back into play. The teams went to the time-out huddles and reset for one last play with the Soviets needing to go the length of the court to score. The in-bounds pass again led to nothing and again the Americans celebrated. Again, the referee was blowing his whistle after noticing the game clock had only been reset to 1.5 seconds. With three seconds back on the clock, the Soviets took their third swing. A long full-court pass found Alexander Belov, who shrugged off two American defenders and scored the basket to win the gold medal for the Soviet Union. It was the first time the US had been beaten in Olympic play since basketball was introduced at Berlin in 1936, ending a streak of 63 straight wins. Believing they had been cheated out of the gold medal, the US team refused to attend the medal ceremony or to receive their silver medals. Those medals remain unclaimed, under lock and key in Europe.

The American players had a choice regarding that loss and their silver medals. They could accept the loss and medals and go home as beaten, but humble and admired athletes. Instead, they chose to protest a result that is still disputed by many almost 50 years later. Unfortunately, 11 Israeli Olympians and one West German police officer had no choice in their final fates. Those 12 men paid the ultimate price through no fault of their own when eight terrorists broke into the athletes' village under the cover of darkness, delivering an awful tragedy that rendered winning and losing into a pale insignificance. Munich 1972 should always be remembered for those who lost their lives trying to live up to the ideals of the Olympic Games.

EDDIE AND THE MEXICANS

Everyone who was anyone would gather at the old Albert Park Stadium on a Wednesday night. They were there to play or watch the state championship games that were the best club basketball contests in Australia. If you wanted to be considered among the best players in the country, Melbourne was the city and Albert Park was the place to prove it. Eddie Palubinskas knew it and he did it.

Born and raised in Canberra, Eddie was a precocious talent. I first saw him at an Australian Championship playing for the Australian Capital Territory against New South Wales. As a rule, ACT was never that good, but this kid kept coming off the bench to keep the game close. Even as a teenager, he was the best player ACT had. My mate Ron Harvey was coaching ACT and every time Eddie would make a few shots to close the gap, Ron would sub him out. After the game, I asked Ron why he kept taking Eddie out of the game. 'We've got to have discipline,' Ron said. Discipline? The only discipline Eddie ever had in his life was his commitment to basketball and making sure he honed his shot as close to perfection as he could imagine.

After he had outgrown Canberra basketball, Eddie moved to Melbourne to play for St Kilda. One Wednesday night he turned up at Albert Park and asked me, 'What's the VBA scoring record?' I told him the number, whatever it was, and he said, 'OK. I'm going to break it tonight'. As good as his word, Eddie went out that night and set a scoring record. That was Eddie in a nutshell.

If he had been born 100 years earlier, Eddie would have been a perfect fit for America's Wild West era. He had the swagger, the confidence and the balls to better Wild Bill Hickock, Wyatt Earp, Butch Cassidy, Jesse James or any other gunslinger. If you challenged Eddie to a shootout on the basketball court, you needed an answered prayer rather than a six-shooter.

The basketball world was introduced to Eddie at the 1972 Munich Olympic Games when he averaged 21.1 points per game as the second-highest scorer for the tournament, still a month short of his 22nd birthday. By the 1974 world championship, everyone knew what to expect. By the 1976 Olympic Games, nobody could really stop him, topping the scoring in Montreal with 31.3 points per game. There was no need to tell Eddie, but it was nice to have a world-class shooter and scorer on the national team.

As we prepared for the 1974 world championship in Puerto Rico, we basically did so without Eddie because he was at college in the United States. He started at Ricks College (now Brigham Young University-Idaho) before transferring to Louisiana State University to play for legendary coach Dale Brown. I met Dale on our first tour of the US, and we became good friends. If I ever thought we had a player who could compete at the college level, Dale said, tell him and he would look after it. Eddie was the first player I recommended.

As it turned out, Baton Rouge, the home of LSU, was our first stop on the way to Puerto Rico and Dale had used his influence to make sure we were accommodated at the best hotel in the city, a welcome relief after 30 hours of travel. Although born in the north, Dale was a man of great southern hospitality, inviting me into his home and proudly showing off the pistol in his wife's bedside dresser, just in case of a burglar. Having built LSU into an excellent basketball program, Dale was coach for 25 years and essentially became the most important man on campus. Dropping into his office one day, I could hear Dale in the middle of a robust telephone conversation with the LSU athletic director. The AD was worried Dale was blowing his budget. 'How can I be overspending the budget,' Dale countered, 'when I don't have a budget?' End of conversation.

After two exhibition games – one just over the state border in Mississippi and one in Baton Rouge – we headed for Puerto Rico with an unexpected upgrade to first-class. Never known to turn down a free drink, our travelling officials and media made sure to make the most of the flowing wine up the front of the plane and were a little wobbly, to say the least, as we collected our bags and headed for the hotel.

While the officials and media cleared their heads, the rest of us got ready to play the USSR in a pre-tournament game. Facing the 1972 Olympic gold medal team was always going to be a tough ask, especially with the Soviets' size advantage. Ray Tomlinson was our starting centre, but the smallest player on the USSR team was as tall as Ray. Even though Rocky Crosswhite was a little taller than Ray, he did not have a typical inside game and preferred short jump shots rather than lay-ups or post moves towards the basket. Conversely, Brian Kerle rarely took a shot outside the key, which was not a good thing against the Soviets given they had that area covered. We ended up losing by about 30 and even one of the Russian referees offered some advice. When Ray complained about some overtly physical action by his Soviet opponent, the referee simply replied, 'You must learn to be tough'. He was right.

The loss to the Soviets was not great for morale and we had a few concerns about trying to find the right blend of players on the floor. As always, we were undersized, and some players were not really multifunctional or made for dual roles. One problem appeared solved when we played Puerto Rico in an exhibition game. The use of Andy Blicavs and Richard Duke in the forward spots looked good and Eddie slipped easily into the role of main scorer. The venue was packed with about 4,000 rabid fans, which, without air conditioning, only made the heat and humidity seem a lot worse than the trial it already was. Only Brian Kerle, a Queensland native, seemed happy and able to handle the conditions, although Eddie soon adapted on his way to a 40-point game.

As the travelling team overseas, there was always the possibility of being on the wrong end of a dodgy call late in the game. This time it was a foul called on Ray Tomlinson as he drove to the basket. The ref somehow awarded Puerto Rico two free-throws – and that cost us victory. I complained to the referee and he said, 'Look around us. We both need to get out of here alive'. I did look around and agreed with him, so no further complaints from me. But leaving the court to a generous ovation from the home fans, we felt good heading into the tournament.

That feeling of optimism turned out to be fool's gold. Drawn in Group C with Canada, Cuba and Czechoslovakia, we lost all three games, but we certainly were in each game and had chances to win. In fact, we were tied with Czechoslovakia inside the last minute only to lose by five. We opened the crossover section of the tournament with an easy win over Central African Republic before closing with three games decided by a total margin of four points. We lost a shootout against the Philippines 101-100 in a frenzied finish that was capped with the winning basket on the buzzer; we beat Argentina 102-100 in another high-scoring contest; and fell to Mexico 85-84 to finish 12th of 14 teams.

It was a disappointing outcome for Australia after we had done well in Munich two years earlier, and I honestly struggled to make a clear or logical assessment of our overall performance. If anything, it was surely not the fault of the players. The lack of adequate international competition in the lead-up to the tournament was probably the difference between finishing in the top-eight and finishing 12th. New guys Andy Blicavs, John Maddock and Ken Burbridge justified selection; there was never an issue with Glenn Marsland and Mark Lampshire, who were great team men despite being stuck on the bench; and the veteran big men did well enough against the odds. While he finished third in scoring for the tournament, Eddie was an enigma. Filling the basket was one thing, but he was too often a defensive liability. He had missed most of our pre-tournament preparation and, looking ahead to the 1976 Olympics, I promised never again to select a player who could not commit to the entire preparation.

That, of course, is much easier said than done. There are always injuries to contend with and players still had to work full-time, making basketball a secondary priority, perhaps even further down the totem pole. But we were at least able to address the matter of more games for the squad before we settled on the final 12 to go to Montreal. Prior to selection, we toured America with seven games in eight days against Pac-8 Conference colleges and had two games in China on the way home. We also had a three-game Olympic qualifying series against New Zealand, sweeping the Tall Blacks by an average of almost 30 points.

Back in Australia, we played two touring teams – one professional, one college – which provided some challenges away from the basketball court. The visiting Belgium All-Stars sounded good, but it was an interesting concept trying to promote the team when nine of the 10 players were Americans who had been playing in Belgium. Two of the Americans had played for clubs in Melbourne before moving to Belgium. As for Mississippi State University, it is fair to say that tour provided ample evidence that basketball players might receive a college education, but that does not make them smart.

As part of the tour, Mississippi State played in Adelaide and took in the local sights – and then took more than the local sights. A colleague from Adelaide called to tell me one of the players had been arrested for robbing a bank. Mild panic set in as he divulged some of the details involved with the heist. Apparently, the player in question went to the bank to cash some traveller's cheques. While the bank teller left the counter to organise the transaction, the player allegedly reached over and grabbed a wad of cash from the open drawer, making a fast break for the exit. Security cameras and silent alarms alerted police to the situation and, soon enough, he was apprehended. Even without the cameras and alarms, it would not have been hard to locate a tall black man in Adelaide in the mid-1970s, especially given an American basketball team was in town.

As the Mississippi State tour was my responsibility, I quickly got on the phone to a friend who had good legal connections in Adelaide. The advice came back soon enough. 'If they have not confiscated his passport,' the friend relayed, 'get him out of the country'. When questioned by the police, the player denied the allegations, no money was found, and they did not ask for his passport. Within 24 hours, the player was on a plane home and the rest of the Mississippi State team completed the tour. There were repercussions in the US, where two or three players transferred the following season and the coach was not far behind.

Throughout the Australian squad's US tour and games at home, we tested out players who could help us overcome our height deficiency at international level. In the end, we went with Andy Campbell and Peter Walsh on the 1976 team, giving us plenty of height even if some questioned their ability. Standing 215cm, Andy was probably our tallest Olympian until Luc Longley in 1988, and Peter was 214cm and known to all as *Grasshopper*, a nickname bestowed by a fellow student after seeing this tangle of arms and legs in his green high school blazer.

Both players were good guys, and *Grasshopper* was always good for a humorous yarn, showing the gift of the gab when he needed to. On arrival in Montreal, *Grasshopper* realised he had left his camera in Australia. He arranged to have it sent to him, only to learn of an excessive customs charge at the Canadian end. Relaying this story to someone in the village precinct, *Grasshopper* may have slightly exaggerated his plight, but a stranger took pity and paid the cost of the tax on the camera.

The seven-footers were two of eight first-time Olympians on the team along with Robbie Cadee, Tony Barnett, Andy Blicavs, Michael Tucker, Russel Simon and John Maddock. The returning veterans were Ian Watson, Eddie Palubinskas, Rocky Crosswhite and Ray Tomlinson. But this was not an inexperienced team given several players had also been at the world titles in Puerto Rico two years previously, so we did go into the Olympic tournament with some decent expectations of a good performance, even with a horrendous schedule. Drawn in Group A, we were pooled with the USSR, Canada, Cuba, Mexico and Japan, needing to finish first or second to advance to the medal round.

The opening two games could not have been tougher, scheduled to play the 1972 gold medal-winning Soviet Union, and Munich bronze medallist Cuba. A 111-89 loss to Cuba was followed by a relatively honourable loss to the Soviets, 93-77. But the most memorable, and historic, game was next up against Mexico. We had identified the Mexico game as crucial for Australia if we were to finish in the top eight places and achieve our highest ever finish at an Olympic Games. After two losses to open the tournament, we needed something special and it was the perfect stage and setting for Eddie Palubinskas.

After doing so well at the Munich Olympics and the worlds in Puerto Rico, Eddie was probably at the peak of his game and the height of his career. Having finished his two years with Dale Brown at LSU, Eddie was chosen by the Atlanta Hawks with the 61st pick of the 1974 NBA draft, and at No.78 by the Utah Stars of the rival American Basketball Association. Despite his ability to shoot the basketball, Eddie never played in either league and the Montreal Olympics were to become his defining moment and farewell to basketball at the highest level.

The game plan against Mexico was to place a major emphasis and premium on defence, keying on shooters Manuel Raga and Arturo Guerrero by overplaying and denying Raga the ball, but pressuring and double-teaming Guerrero as soon as he caught the ball. The strategy was so good that Raga finished with 24 points and Guerrero had 40. Despite our desire and willingness to play defence, we were caught in the middle of a serious shootout and trailed by one point, 58-57, at the half.

My coaching style has often been described as an imitation of General Custer. No matter how many of the enemy were coming over the ridge at the Battle of Little Bighorn, Custer refused to change strategy. The stubborn strategy led to the battle also being known as Custer's Last Stand: he was killed and the 7th Cavalry Regiment under his command was badly defeated.

But I knew at half-time of this game we needed to go basket-for-basket with Mexico if we were to win because we sure as hell weren't able to stop them, given they were shooting at 74 per cent from the field. Fortunately, we had Eddie Palubinksas and he revelled in the circumstances with one of the all-time great Olympic performances. The game finished 107-107 at the end of regulation before Australian won in overtime, 120-117. The total of 237 points remains the highest aggregate score in Olympic history and Eddie had an amazing 48 of them.

While Mexico cooled off, Australia kept on going, hitting an outstanding 67.1 per cent from the field as Tony Barnett, Andy Blicavs, Michael Tucker and Rocky Crosswhite all scored in double figures to support Eddie. In fact, Andy Blicavs shot a perfect 9-9 from the field for his 19 points, a brilliant performance overshadowed by Eddie, who went 20-24 from the field and 8-10 from the free-throw line. To cap things off, Eddie released an audibly loud, gut-wrenching belch followed by a cartwheel into a handspring at the opposite end of the court as we sealed the game from the free-throw line. Eddie was nothing if not a showman.

An easy win over Japan clinched fourth place in Group A, meaning we could not finish worse than eighth, and that was exactly where we finished after classification losses to Italy by seven, and to Cuba by 11. We led Italy by as much as 14, but an injury to Tony Barnett proved a turning point and we could not stay the pace with Cuba in our final game. We had achieved our goal of Australia's best Olympic finish by taking eighth place. But we could have and should have done better and, on reflection, I was guilty of a serious error of judgment.

Our entire build-up to the Olympic Games had been focused on finishing as high as possible, but within the top-eight. Once the draw was done, we focused on Mexico as the key game to achieve that outcome. Having thought about it quite often, I realise I should have set a different and much higher target. We should have been ambitious and aimed at winning a medal. At that stage, Australia's international basketball standing did not warrant such goals, and anybody would have plainly said it was unrealistic for us to win a medal at the 1976 Olympics. But had we raised our expectations and been able to generate the same relentless approach we had against Mexico in the games against Cuba, Canada and Italy, maybe those losses become victories and we would be in medal contention. People have scoffed at that notion when I have mentioned it, believing we should have been considered lucky just to be at the Olympics. Just being there was and is not enough. We should have gone there aiming for a medal.

If there was one overall victory at Montreal, it was that Eddie Palubinskas topped the tournament scoring with an average of 31.3 points per game, shooting at a remarkable 56.9 per cent from the field. After starting with 28 points against Cuba, Eddie had games of 29, 48, 28, 30, 30 and 26. After finishing second in scoring at Munich, it would not surprise me if Eddie had set himself the target of topping all scorers at Montreal. That was the kind of confidence and self-belief Eddie had. It was just like the night Eddie walked into Albert Park and declared he would break the VBA scoring record right there, that night. Eddie believed he was one of the best shooters and scorers in the world, and, whether it was Albert Park Stadium or the Montreal Forum, he went out and proved it.

SEVEN-POINT SPREAD

There were about five minutes left in the game and the margin was at 13 points. Sitting next to me was Bob Staunton and Al Ramsey. I said to them, 'I think we're in trouble here'. It wasn't that I could see into the future, but the gnawing feeling in the pit of my stomach told me I was right, and it was confirmed as Italy and Cuba managed the game down to the buzzer. They made sure they got the only result that enabled both teams to advance at the 1980 Olympic Games and stopped Australia from doing so.

It has not been uncommon to hear stories of match-fixing in basketball, especially in regions where betting on games is rife. Certainly, there were times during games, or immediately after games, that you understand why certain calls are made by referees to balance the margin or maybe get the home team over the line against a foreign club. It is perhaps best referred to as result management rather than match-fixing. To be too obvious would be to risk detection.

This defining game for Australia at the Moscow Olympics – a game we were not even playing in – was certainly managed over the closing minutes, but to say it was fixed would be wrong and preposterous. It would be more accurate to say there was a gentlemen's agreement with nothing more than a knowing nod and a wink between Cuba and Italy to make sure both teams got what they wanted – in this case a place in the medal rounds at Australia's expense.

After opening the tournament with an 83-76 loss to Cuba, we came back with an 84-77 win over Italy, one of the best performances by Australia in an Olympic campaign to that point. With Dino Meneghin at centre and Pierluigi Marzorati considered one of the world's best playmakers, Italy was a formidable opponent. But Phil Smyth did a job on Marzorati, and Larry Sengstock did very well against Meneghin. In fact, they both did so well, an Italian shirt-fronted Phil away from the ball in a bid to end his involvement, and Meneghin's frustration spilled over and he was assessed a technical foul.

Gracious in defeat, Italy's coach told the media: 'Australia had courage, determination, pride and they laid their guts on the floor'. But within 48 hours, Italy's coach would have the last say on Australia's bid to make the medal round for the first time at an Olympic Games.

A win over Sweden would certainly put us in the box seat to advance in first or second place from Group C with either Cuba or Italy. After leading Sweden 40-27 at half-time, we were the victims of self-inflicted wounds in the second half. Our shooting percentage went to hell and we managed to score just 25 points for the period, winning 64-55. That final margin and ordinary second half was to come back and bite us hard as Cuba and Italy took to the floor at the CSKA Sports Palace with only one outcome that would eliminate us from the medal round. Because of the nature of the results, standings and tiebreakers, that outcome had to be a seven-point win for Italy. Nothing else would hurt us.

All was going to plan as Italy led Cuba by one at the break and then opened a double-digit margin. But as the gap got out to 13 and Italy missed a free-throw, the dread started rising from my toes up into my body. That was when I told Bob and Al to be ready for what was about to happen. Neither Bob nor Al would have any of it. They thought I was nuts, but I had been to enough major tournaments to know how things can play out. Sure enough, Italy's lead gradually reduced to 11, to nine and finally to seven, leaving both teams to manage the game over the closing minutes. It was gut-wrenching, to say the least. Given any margin except seven would have worked for us, it was interesting to note Italy's performance from the free-throw line against Cuba. Other than the game against Cuba, Italy converted its free-throws at 71.2 per cent for the tournament. Against Cuba, Italy was 19-38 from the line – an unimpressive 50 per cent – and Meneghin was 1-6. There is absolutely no suggestion Italy or any of the players deliberately missed free-throws against Cuba to stage the result. It is simply a presentation of the statistics.

Of course, had Australia scored one more basket against Sweden and allowed one fewer score by the Scandinavians, the Cuba-Italy game would have been rendered irrelevant to our chances of advancing. That is where that poor second half against Sweden, a late inclusion to the tournament because of the Olympic boycott by several countries, came back to hurt. Officials needed to imple-ment a third tiebreaker to split Italy, Cuba and Australia and we missed out by the slimmest margin. Under different tie-breaking methods we would have gone through to the medal round. But it was not to be with seven our unlucky number.

The lead-up to the Moscow Olympics was dominated by news and debate surrounding which countries would boycott the

Games after the Soviet Union invaded Afghanistan. The USSR backed the Afghanistan government, but trouble flared in 1979 with the assassination of the country's leader. Needing to assert its authority and presence in the face of rising civil unrest, the USSR went into Afghanistan and installed a Soviet loyalist as president. It was a move that split world opinion and created a massive divide through the Olympic movement, causing repercussions for the 1980 and 1984 Games. Of 146 countries invited to the Moscow Olympics, 66 – including the United States, Canada and China - declined and stayed home, and seven nations opted not to march at the opening ceremony. The 80 countries at the Olympics were the fewest since 1956 in Melbourne.

The Australian Government, with Malcolm Fraser as Prime Minister, was strongly in favour of boycotting the Moscow Olympics and applied pressure on the Australian Olympic Committee, as an organisation, and athletes, as individuals. Urged by the US to boycott the Games, Fraser would not make a unilateral decision to block the AOC or athletes attending, but his lobbying was intense. Eventually, the AOC executive decided – after a split vote – to attend the Moscow Olympics. Several athletes decided to stay home, and Australia competed under the Olympic flag. Having supported one of Australian sport's most important initiatives after the Montreal Games in 1976, Prime Minister Fraser wanted nothing to do with the 1980 Olympics.

The 1976 Games were an unmitigated disaster for the Australian Olympic team overall. The medal return was one silver – by the men's hockey team – and four bronze – two in sailing, one in swimming and one in equestrian. It was the first time since 1936 Australia had failed to win an Olympic gold medal and was just four years after 17 total medals – including eight gold – at Munich. The pressure applied from the sporting community and organisations about lack of government funding for Olympic sports forced a move. The federal government, finally acting on reports and recommendations that had been started and made in the early to mid-1970s, backed the establishment of the Australian Institute of Sport in Canberra. The fruits of the AIS, opened in 1981, would take time to be savoured, but basketball was able to move on from 1976 with its own game-changing funding package.

Part of my job as Victorian Basketball Association general manager still entailed manning the door at Albert Park Stadium to collect the entry cost for training and playing. I was usually only on duty long enough to greet the early arrivals. But one day I was there long enough to be drawn into a conversation about the Olympics, Australia's results and what we needed to ensure a better result for the basketball team at Moscow in 1980. I had already furnished a report to the Australian Basketball Federation and I told this well-meaning lower-grade player exactly the same. Basically, we needed more funding to enable more training, more games, more help. With that, he was gone, heading down to the back courts for a game.

About a week later, I was invited to a meeting with a marketing company representing Tattersalls, the lottery giant that now generates billions of dollars in winnings and revenue every year. The midweek player I had chatted to worked with the marketing agency. By talking to me, he was getting a feel for basketball's situation heading towards the next Olympics, knowing Tattsersalls wanted to sponsor at least one major sporting organisation. The decision came down to hockey or basketball, two sports that had done well at Montreal with the prospect of doing better at Moscow. After submissions from the Australian Basketball Federation, Tattersalls agreed to sponsor the national team through to the 1980 Olympics. The sponsorship, the largest for basketball to that point, was a major boost for the sport and the national team. It was a sponsorship that allowed us to do things with the national team that we had wanted to do for a long time as we prepared for the 1978 world championship in the Philippines and 1980 Olympics in Moscow.

We quickly established the Tattersalls Test Series, essentially a sponsorship name for tours by the best international teams we could bring to Australia. While the primary aim was to give the national team more exposure to quality opposition, we also included club teams on the touring teams' schedules so the experience filtered down to those who would not get the chance to play for Australia. During 1978, there were tours by Czechoslovakian club Slavia Prague, Canadian college Simon Fraser University and, significantly, the United States national team as a final warm-up for both teams ahead of the world championship.

Although Australia lost all seven games to the US, there was reason for optimism after losing two matches by one point and four points, and the other defeats in the range of 11 to 18 points. The only real negative to come out of the series was an injury to Tony Forbes. A young player who could score, Forbes was involved in a nasty collision during the second game against the US and was diagnosed with a chipped vertebra. It was an injury that suddenly jeopardised his place in the team for the Philippines. Given we didn't have much time before the world championship, a quick decision had to be made. Medical advice indicated he would recover and there was minimal risk of more damage. All Tony needed was a decent dose of painkiller before each game.

In fact, Tony was one of nine players making their debuts for Australia at a major event. The other first-timers were Mel Dalgleish, Gordie McLeod, Phil Smyth, Larry Sengstock, Les Riddle, Danny Morseau, Ric Hodges and Steve Gray. The returnees were Andy Blicavs, John Maddock and Peter Walsh. It was a team built of grit and determination rather than flat-out talent, and a man who came to epitomise that was Dalgleish. An undersized big-man, Dalgleish was playing for Dandenong Rangers, coached by my brother Tony, and was somewhat fortunate to make the team after centre Andy Campbell withdrew. On scholarship at Louisiana State University with coach Dale Brown, Campbell was suffering back problems, forcing him to pull out. It turned out the inclusion of Dalgleish was a bonus for us as he relished the defensive assignments to cover quality players. At 6'5", Mel was not big by international standards, but he played aggressively and physically within the rules and was the type of player everyone loved to play with and hated to play against.

That kind of Dalgleish attitude and approach was one we all needed in Manila, where the tournament was split between two venues: 28,000-seat Areneta Coliseum with air conditioning, and 10,000-seat Rizal Stadium without air conditioning. We played only two of our 10 games – the first and last – at the Areneta, which had hosted the *Thriller in Manila* between Muhammad

Ali and Joe Frazier three years earlier. We were made to swelter in the Rizal for the other eight games, making them a test of endurance, determination, and survival against the elements. It was just as big a test against our Group C opposition: United States, Czechoslovakia and Dominican Republic, three teams we had never beaten in major international competition.

The status quo remained against the US in our opening game of the tournament, but only just. We led throughout the first half before the Americans opened an 11-point game in the second half. Typical of this young and inexperienced group, we fought back and went toe-to-toe with the Americans and only a couple of missed opportunities left us short, losing 77-75. With Phil Smyth and Andy Blicavs leading the scoring, Australia had exposed the US and gained some real confidence with a performance that took us to the brink of a major upset in world championship history.

The heat and humidity inside Rizal Stadium were equally as formidable opponents as Czechoslovakia in our second game. Our defence and the relentless presence of our big bodies – Larry Sengstock, Steve Gray, Peter Walsh, Ric Hodges and Mal Dalgleish – were key factors as we went basket-for-basket in the second half to win 81-78. That victory meant a win over Dominican Republic would send us into the second round and a chance of a medal.

We led the Dominicans by 11 points at halftime, but that margin was quickly shrinking against a zone defence in the second period. With the game heading towards a turning point, I called on Tony Forbes for the first time. We had not played him in the first two games to ensure his neck injury improved, but now we needed to make sure we did not lose the initiative. It was something of a gamble to put Tony in the game and I gave him an instruction I had never given any player before or since: 'I want you to shoot the ball every time you receive it anywhere in the front court'. The look on Tony's face was stunned amazement, but I reiterated my instruction that he had a licence to shoot. With the first chance he got, Tony launched a long-range shot. It connected and it was the only basket Tony scored in that game, but it was like our offence was freed of the Dominican shackles, allowing us to hold on for a 74-72 win and a place in the next round.

Over the years, the tournament formats of the world championship and Olympic Games have varied. In 1978, the top two teams from three groups advanced to the medal round, joining host Philippines and Olympic gold medallist Russia for a final-eight. It was another round-robin with each team playing six games while skipping the team from your qualifying group. Even though we did not have to face the US again, it was a brutal schedule and one that showed us what it was like – and what Australia needed – to compete in the top tier of international basketball.

After a hammering from the Soviet Union, we took another heavy loss from Brazil due to a costly first-half lapse, giving up 59 points, and there were two more defeats against Italy and Canada by reduced margins. We ended that four-game losing streak with a strong win over Philippines and then pushed Yugoslavia all the way in a 105-101 loss. Already qualified for the gold medal game, Yugoslavia took a cautious approach and the coach used his starters sparingly in the first half. That mattered little to us and we took the game at Yugoslavia as though it was the gold medal game. Although we were down by 15 at halftime, we continued to play hard and closed the gap with a 60-49 second half, giving ourselves a chance of winning. It was a complete team effort from Australia with all 12 players scoring and six hitting double-digits. But perhaps the most interesting statistic was Australia being called for 36 fouls to Yugoslavia's 19, while Yugoslavia was 35-43 from the free-throw line to Australia's 15-19. An extra 20 points from free-throws is more than enough in a four-point game.

Our final game of the tournament was another easy win over Philippines, claiming seventh place and Australia's best finish at a world championship. The gold medal went to Yugoslavia with an overtime victory against the Soviet Union, and Brazil claimed bronze ahead of Italy to close a fascinating tournament in a fascinating country that can really boast basketball as a religion. If that is considered an overstatement, consider the front page of one of Manila's daily newspapers in the lead-up to the world championship. After Philippines had beaten Puerto Rico in a warm-up game, the headline was *P.I. 5 RIPS P.R.* At the bottom of the page was *Pope dies. See page 4.*

Between the 1978 worlds and the 1980 Olympics there was a significant move for Australian basketball with the formation of the National Basketball League, which made its debut in 1979 and developed into a quality, full-time professional competition. It was a move made with the idea of improving players, the standard of Australian basketball and the profile of the sport. But the bottom line was everyone was still essentially an amateur and still had to work for a living. We were also heading towards the final year of the Tattersalls sponsorship and we made sure to make the most of it for the national team with a busy schedule and preparation for the 1980 Olympics. But the closer we got towards the Moscow Games, the more the doubts rose about whether we would be allowed to attend.

During and after the final selection camps for Moscow, few thought we would be going to the Olympics as Prime Minister Malcolm Fraser increased his call to join the United States in boy-cotting as protest of the Soviet Union invasion of Afghanistan. It was an issue that split the country and various sporting bodies and individuals. As the basketball delegate to the Victorian Olympic Committee, I was nowhere near being involved in any deci-sion-making process but had a feeling our state executive wanted to go to the Olympics. The only concern among the VOC about voting in favour of going to the Games was being shunned when it came to future government funding.

Even when the AOC finally voted 6-5 to attend the Olympics, the Prime Minister took a different angle and called on individ-uals to examine their consciences and withdraw. Some athletes did decide to boycott the Games, and I was disappointed by that stance, as well as the political pressure that was applied. But I was also duty-bound to offer every player selected for the Olympic basketball team the opportunity, or at least to consider the oppor-tunity, to withdraw if they felt so inclined. None of the players declined selection.

The selection of the national team is a most difficult task and I was always conscious of the immense responsibility I had. It was more than choosing a team for one tournament. It was under-standing and knowing how my choices could impact on a player's life and career. That was especially so in Olympic years because there is no such thing as a former Olympian. Once you are an Olympian, you are an Olympian for life, and that is a rich and tremendous honour to have. In 1980, there was a concern that those named to their first Olympics may be non-Olympians if the government had forced through the Moscow boycott.

Seven players from the 1978 world championship team – Mel Dalgleish, Gordie McLeod, Phil Smyth, Larry Sengstock, Les Riddle, Danny Morseu and Peter Walsh – carried over to 1980, we brought back Rocky Crosswhite and Michael Tucker from the 1976 team, and we named Peter Ali, Steve Breheny and Ian Davies for their first major event.

Of the new players, Davies was the wildcard. Born in Tasmania, Davies was the son of former Carlton footballer Fred Davies. When Fred died just before his 40th birthday, his widow took Ian to the United States for a new life and a path into basketball. After four seasons at Graceland College, an NAIA school playing below NCAA standard, Davies was recruited by Launceston's NBL team for the 1980 season. During the process, Launceston believed Ian was an American, but was delighted to find out he was in fact an Australian, thus giving it the right to sign another American recruit. That was good for Launceston and proved to be a bonus for the Australian national team. No shot was out of range for Davies, making him difficult to guard and enjoyable to watch. It also made him an automatic selection for Australia.

As we started the warm-up games for Moscow, the spectre of a boycott still loomed large and it may have affected our mindset and our play. That seemed to be the case as we laboured to beat a touring team from Oklahoma in Adelaide, where the atmosphere was hardly responsive. The die-hard basketball fans of Adelaide have never forgiven me for not picking Werner Linde for the national team. A brilliant shooter and former Australian teammate, Linde was a South Australian idol. But Phil Smyth had quickly emerged as the new basketball hero from the *City of Churches* and his contributions for the national team were valuable over a long period, especially as an Olympic rookie at Moscow.

On the eve of our series against Yugoslavian club side Jugoplastika, the name derived from the sponsor of the Split-based team, the decision regarding the Moscow boycott arrived. The AOC voted to attend the Olympic Games, the announcement reaching the national team in mid-air when the pilot of our aircraft relayed the decision. The reaction of the passengers was rather muted with spattered applause. I didn't know if the reaction was apathy or inhibition, or whether it was only our players clapping. After the Jugoplastika series, we had two games against the University of Puget Sound, the alma mater of former Melbourne Tigers and St Kilda Saints import David Lindstrom. Those games were supposed to top off our Olympic preparation, but they basically occurred amid panic and chaos.

As we reached Devonport for the first game against UPS, word had reached us that Prime Minister Fraser was trying to recall the AOC executive in a bid to reverse its decision. The Prime Minister was trying to bully through a boycott. That was enough for our team manager Bob Staunton to become stressed beyond belief, but also to think and perform remarkably well under the circumstances. Worried about government intervention, Bob started working on changing our travel plans so we could leave Australia ahead of schedule. If we were out of the country, it would be a lot harder getting us back than stopping us from leaving. Even some of the state basketball federations were starting to back a boycott, so we got out of town a week early, heading for Moscow via Germany and Yugoslavia.

During three days in Munich, we managed to get in six solid training sessions, a surprise meeting with FIBA secretary-general William Jones and a visit to the famous Hofbrauhauss, where previous patrons had included Wolfgang Amadeus Mozart, Vladimir Lenin and Adolf Hitler as he plotted his rise to power in Nazi Germany. With no sightings of the famous or otherwise, the main thing worth noting was the strength and agility of the waitresses as they navigated the crowd of drinkers while carrying the massive steins of beer.

From Munich we went to Yugoslavia, where the balls were never fully inflated, the nets were tight and the referees were homers, which meant we had to work for every basket we could get. But there were no excuses for our performance in the first game in Sibenik, where 30 turnovers came from bad passes and another six came from players simply stepping out of bounds. The games we played against the Yugoslavia national team ended with embarrassing losses on the scoreboard, but the experience of playing against some of the world's best players was invaluable.

On arrival in Moscow, we were pleasantly surprised to find the village accommodation better than we had expected. It was two men to a room and close to restaurants and shops. It was a good start and Bob Staunton got in early to deliver his reminder of what was required from the players when representing Australia. Everyone had heard Bob's speech or similar before, but the team manager was quite stern in his delivery about good conduct and punctuality. His closing remarks were a warning about the local women. According to Bob's intel, there was a high risk of catching a sexually transmitted disease while fraternising with the locals, and he recommended against it.

No sooner had Bob finished, than Ian Davies had a question. 'Are girls allowed in our room?' Such was the deadpan delivery nobody knew if Ian was taking Bob for a ride or if he was deadly serious. Ironically, I read in a local English-language newspaper there was a warning for local citizens to avoid intimate contact with foreigners, believing *they* carried a high incidence of venereal disease. Unfortunately, some players did catch something local: a bug that had them on the toilet more than the basketball court.

Of course, fraternisation between members of the opposite sex was quite common at the Olympic Games, especially when athletes had finished their competitions and had nothing to do except party and fool around. Some members of our Olympic basketball teams over the years were quite handsome and did well with the ladies. On one occasion – and the identity of the individual and the year of the Olympics will remain in the vault to protect the guilty party – a player struck up quite the friendship with a female athlete. The two became close and got amorous one evening in the village. They could not go to his room, nor could they go to hers. So, they opted for a romp in one of the garden beds. Alerted to the rustling bushes, a security guard shone his torch on a couple of bare bums and sheepish-looking athletes. Imagine the guard's reaction when the couple emerged: he a tall gangly Australian basketballer, and she a rather heavyset, squat Bulgarian weightlifter.

One of the greatest servants that Australian basketball has ever had, Bob Staunton always did it hard when it came to keeping players in line. A company man 99 per cent of the time, Bob relayed news that there was a limit on the number of athletes and officials allowed to march at the opening ceremony. Bob was worried about players marching when they shouldn't but I was happy for them to use their initiative. A big part of being an Olympian is to march at the opening ceremony and I felt they should do so if they wished. There was further anguish for Bob when he was told the limit on numbers meant he could not march. It was too much for Bob and he broke down. I told him to march in my place. I had marched before and was happy to watch on TV. But Bob was such a stickler for following orders from HQ, he declined my offer. One abiding memory of the 1980 opening ceremony was the TV cameras zooming into the face of a young boy, smiling brightly and enjoying the occasion. Given I had noticed a distinct absence of children around Moscow while out in the streets, it struck me as odd that TV had been able to pick out this one child among 80,000. Perhaps it was also coincidental the lad was wearing an official identification card hanging around his neck. Propaganda at its finest.

Once basketball actually took precedence over everything else, there were still issues to deal with. One issue was dealing with the training venues. It took an hour each way to the venues, although that time might have been reduced if the drivers knew where they were going. As for the training courts themselves, it was obvious they would be completed *after* the Olympic Games. One of the floors was still raw timber, not sanded and unvarnished. We might as well have been training on asphalt. The new balls we were given were left feeling like sandpaper and basically useless after one training session.

Fortunately, playing the games provided us with a change of outlook and attitude. After a close loss to Cuba, we ran off wins over Italy and Sweden, only to be totally gutted by the result of the managed finish to the Cuba-Italy game. We could have easily let the contents of our suitcase fly all over the road after that result, but the players showed the quality of their character against Czechoslovakia in the first of the crossover games. I will never forget the courage and determination of our players in that game. We won 91-86 as Larry Sengstock battled manfully against much bigger opponents; Ian Davies made a mockery of the Czech defence, an attempted box-and-one, with 36 points; and Phil Smyth played all 40 minutes as a supreme leader.

After a loss to Poland, we won the last two games against Senegal and India to have a 5-2 record, but only finished eighth. Italy went 4-4 and won a silver medal after losing to undefeated Yugoslavia in the final. Our objective had been to reach the top-six and we thought we had done that before the infamous seven-point spread got us. We posted our best Olympic result, but it was the most disappointing Games for me. Off the floor, there are memories of faceless, joyless commuters on the Moscow subway, the absence of children from the city, the rigid authoritarian police control, the queues, the rain, seeing the Moscow Circus, the Bolshoi Ballet and the Moscow Museum of Art.

There was also Bob Staunton's increased stuttering in line with the increase in stress, and there was my decreased understanding of the attitudes of young players, who mainly preferred life in the village to getting out and experiencing an intriguing city. There were also sleepless nights and the looming end to the Tattersalls sponsorship that had done so much to help the national team over the four-year span between Olympics.

Given all that, it was as good a time as any for me to finish. During the tournament, I had decided it was time to step down as national coach. The pressure of the job was gnawing at me, and the amount of time spent on the road left me feeling I was not doing justice to my family or to the role of coach of Melbourne Tigers. I confided my intention to Alan Dawe, my assistant coach on the national team, and asked if he would be a candidate to take over. The question mark on the question had not even settled before Alan declared there was no way he would do the job. With that, I decided to keep my counsel for a few more months and make a decision on the national team in a more sober and rational environment. Or at least until the pain of that seven-point spread had started to subside a little.

NOT BAD FOR A ROOKIE

The team manager's place is usually at the far end of the bench, leaving it only to hand out towels and drink bottles when necessary. But about 10 minutes into Australia's opening game of the 1984 Olympic Games, I sensed our team manager Bob Elphinston leaning in close to my ear. 'Not bad for a rookie,' Bob whispered. They were five words that said and covered everything about the subject he was commenting on.

The subject was Andrew Gaze and his selection for the Los Angeles Olympics. Having just turned 19 as the Olympics opened and the son of the coach, there was much criticism and many accusations of nepotism. Of course, much of that talk was done out of my earshot and behind my back, but there was no question Andrew and I were aware of it.

As Wayne Carroll's backup, Andrew subbed into the opening game against Brazil and immediately made his mark on the Olympics and international basketball. Intercepting a Brazilian pass, Andrew made a quick behind-the-back dribble to get around a defender and drove to the basket for an uncontested layup. That was when Bob was moved to get up from the end of the bench. The interpretation of Bob's five words: He's earned his place.

After that initial basket, Andrew played a key role with Ian Davies and Phil Smyth. All three hit some extraordinary shots from the perimeter as we played manfully, gamely holding our lead to win 76-72, outscoring Brazil 42-34 in the second half. The win setup a decent tournament for us, beating West Germany and Egypt to finish third in Group A for a quarterfinal against Spain. We lost to Spain by eight, 101-93, and were so close to making the medal round, but had to settle for seventh after losing to Uruguay in our first classification game and then beating West Germany again.

The 1984 Olympic campaign again supported the reputation of the Australian men's team as the undersized overachievers, but we had made our presence felt more than before, and Andrew was a key part of that process. During those Olympic Games, Andrew often played more like a veteran than a teenaged rookie.

The 12 months before the LA Olympics demanded that fresh talent be looked at for the national team. As head coach I asked for views and opinions, especially from the coach of the junior national team, Ian Laurie. With an overseas tour planned for 1983, his recommendation was to consider four players: Michael Johnson, Peter Wain, Mark Dalton and Andrew. By the time Olympic selection arrived, Mark and Andrew were in the 12 for LA.

Of that quartet of young players recommended to me, Michael Johnson was the one I have second-guessed myself over for the past 35-or-so years. An excellent shooter with rangy athleticism, Michael was a player who could make an impact, and he proved it in more than 350 NBL games with the Newcastle Falcons. I have often wondered what might have happened had I picked Michael for a major event with the national team, and it surprised me that my successor Adrian Hurley didn't pick him during his tenure, either.

My greatest concern with any selection process is that it must be fair. That is one of the reasons I have never publicly criticised the selection of an Olympic or world championship team since my time as coach. It is the coach's job to choose his 12 players and he needs to do it and stand by it. What people tend to overlook when being critical of selections – and, especially, omissions - is they may not have the full story or know what the coach knows or thinks about a player from the time they have spent together in camps, on tours and at tournaments. Simply consider that those on the inside know more than those on the outside and most of that is never made public.

Which leads to the question of Andrew's selection and whether it was difficult choosing my son ahead of other older, more experienced and – some believed – better players. My answer: Not really. I have no hesitation in saying Andrew, like the other 11 players on the 1984 team, was selected on merit and for what he could bring to the team. In the past there had been a quota system for selection as the bureaucrats insisted on players from every state being in the national team. When I was made coach, I insisted on having a strong element of chemistry and teamwork and the best 12 players for the job.

In the past, national teams were announced at the closing ceremony of the national championship. For me, that was a cruel and horrible way to publicly release the team. It was fine for those who made the team; terrible for those who did not. So, I made sure on my appointment every player involved with the larger squad would receive a letter advising they were in or out before the team was made public. Which was exactly how Andrew found out he was selected for the 1984 Olympics. I never gave a hint one way or the other and he had to wait for his letter from Basketball

Australia just like everyone else. I don't think Andrew was happy that I made him wait, but that was the way it was, whether he or anyone else liked it or not.

People have said often enough that a father-and-son combination as coach-and-player does not work. I disagree and I think history proves me right in the instance of Andrew and me. He was never treated any differently to other players, and they were not treated any differently to him. When asked about it, my explanation is that all my players were all my sons. There is a love for your team and your players and their characters and personalities.

After the 1984 Olympics, only those with extremely critical attitudes wanted to find something wrong with Andrew's selection and performance. For the majority, it was accepted, begrudgingly or otherwise. But I had seen Andrew playing like that for several seasons with the Tigers, so I knew exactly what he was capable of.

One of the first times I had an inkling of what Andrew was capable of came in a VBA Championship grand final against Geelong. As I recall, Geelong was stacked with talent, including Cal Bruton and James Crawford. We were ahead in a tight game. Brian Goorjian ran the point and got fouled out. Bruce Palmer moved into that role but made a mess of it. So, I put Andrew in, he steadied the ship and saved the game for us. He was only about 16 and playing against NBL opposition. Imagine putting a kid in that situation now. The key was that Andrew had the basketball ability, skills, IQ and maturity to handle it.

That became the hallmark of Andrew's game over his career. What do you need to be a good pro? You need to be able to do your job and get it done when it counts. For the Tigers, for teams overseas, and for the Boomers, Andrew continually got the job done at a high level.

During one of his visits to Australia, Paul Westhead, who coached the LA Lakers to an NBA championship, told me he was going to watch a game and study Andrew intently to learn what he does. So, Andrew played, scored about 40 points, and Paul said he still didn't know how he did it. People would watch a game and think Andrew had scored 20. He would have had 38 or 40. Andrew was never spectacular or had the wow factor. He was efficient and smart with backdoor plays, layups, high-percentage shots in the flow of the offence. Those characteristics took time for others to recognise, but they were why I believe Andrew could have had an NBA career.

After the 1988 Olympic Games, Andrew played a season of college ball with Seton Hall, making the final of the National Collegiate Athletic Association Tournament. That in itself was a watershed moment for Australian basketball and Seton Hall. The whole thing was an achievement against the odds for such a small school, and it gained plenty of media attention in the US and Australia. Even Australian television picked it up as a significant event, thanks to the wisdom of Ron Casey, the long-time Channel 7 general manager in Melbourne. While Ron's two main sporting loves were football and boxing, he was a tremendous supporter of basketball, finding a few minutes here and there on the Sunday *World of Sport* program for me to talk about games, players and coaches. As much as I lobbied Ron for games to be telecast, and as much as he wanted to help, he often reminded me, 'Lindsay, we can live without basketball'. It was his way of saying football was the main priority for TV. But Ron decided to show the 1989 NCAA Final live at about noon on a Tuesday, and he called me with the news. 'I wanted you to be the first to know,' he said. It was a bold move and paid off as the game rated better than the popular *Mike Walsh Show* on a rival station.

After leaving Seton Hall, Andrew went to preseason camp with the Seattle SuperSonics and was the last man cut. A few years later he had two 10-day contracts with the Washington Bullets, and, later still, a lockout-shortened season with the San Antonio Spurs as they went on to win the NBA championship.

There were several other opportunities for Andrew to go to the NBA, or at least training camps and preseasons, but he was mostly reluctant to leave the Tigers in the middle of the NBL season or be unavailable for the national team. The one chance I felt he should have taken was with the Boston Celtics. Dave Gavitt, the former Big East commissioner, knew Andrew from his time at Seton Hall and had become the general manager of the Celtics. He called and said he wanted Andrew to go to training camp. He said there was no guarantee of a job but intimated a spot on the roster was available unless he was a total disaster during the pre-season. I encouraged Andrew to go to Boston because I believed he could be a good NBA player in the right circumstances, and I felt the Celtics were presenting the right circumstances. But Andrew declined and it was a good opportunity missed.

At the end of it all, the NBA wasn't Andrew's dream. He had other priorities such as the Tigers and the Australian team. If he had an absolute passion to be in the NBA, Andrew would have taken those opportunities as they arose. There was no doubt he enjoyed his NBA experiences, and there are no what-ifs or could-have-beens left floating on the breeze.

There were two sojourns in Europe, one with Udine in Italy and another with Apollon Patras in Greece, and Andrew did well during both. There was a game during his season with Udine that summed up Andrew's ability to cope with various teams, leagues and whatever strategies were employed. I was visiting him and watched a game where Udine would struggle if Andrew or the other import were off the court. Sensing the situation, Andrew took charge of the team on the court and took over the game. The coach had not told him to change roles mid-game. He just did it almost instinctively and he stayed in that role for the rest of the season, going from player to leader. Regardless of what the stats might say, Andrew had the ability to play well at whatever the level of the competition. He could always raise his game.

Even though we worked together as coach and player for something like 25 years – maybe more – Andrew and I never clashed or disagreed to the point of conflict. I was usually calm and relaxed, and Andrew was often emotional and excitable. It was probably a good balance to have and our relationship as coach and player endured until we both retired from the Tigers and the NBL at the end of the 2004-05 season. On his exit, Andrew was the NBL's all-time leading scorer, and won the MVP award seven times, among numerous honours.

It has long been said that Andrew was Australia's greatest ever basketballer. For me, those comments and assessments are water off a duck's back. For me, such titles exist only momentarily because there is always going to be someone to overtake what you have done. It is fair to commend and recognise achievements in one particular era, but comparing eras is invalid. There are sportspeople from one era who were good and beat their opposition, but they may not have done so in another era. It is simply enough to be admired.

Which brings to mind a quote: 'There is no great satisfaction in being better than someone else.' The real achievement is being better than you have been in the past. I think Andrew was able to achieve that. Every day when he stepped onto the practice court, he strived to be better than he was the day before. That was what made him the player he was.

It was an attitude and work ethic that took him to five Olympic Games, including Sydney 2000 when he led the Australian team into the stadium as flag bearer for the opening ceremony. Not even the most optimistic among us would have predicted a career that included five Olympics, not even when Bob Elphinston wandered from one end of the bench to the other to whisper in my ear, 'Not bad for a rookie'.

SAY A LITTLE PRAYER

My mother always wanted the best for her three sons. Unfortunately, that included sending us to Sunday school. Although my mother was not a churchgoer herself, she felt an obligation that Barry, Tony and I should at least be exposed to the Christian faith. So, every Sunday morning, she would dress us in our best clothes and send us off to the local church. It was a lost cause almost from the beginning. After a few lessons from the Bible, we decided there were better things to do on Sunday mornings. Even though we dressed for church and headed in that direction, we each had our bathing togs on under our Sunday best and would divert to the pool in the park across the street, sneaking into swim rather than learn about forgiving our sins.

By the time the three of us were teenagers, religion was essentially dismissed as we developed agnostic views that were strengthened by discussions with our uncle Clem, an amazingly smart man and serious philosopher. I have not read the Bible front-to-back, but I have read extracts, and, like other works of fiction, I have difficulty coming to grips with some of the things written. Some of the philosophy is spot-on, such as don't kill your neighbours, but that is really just common sense. That said, I've never riled against religion. A few Mormons have tried to convert me. 'You are so close,' they would say. 'You don't drink, smoke or gamble.' But I will always remember a conversation with Ken James, an American Mormon who played for Melbourne Tigers. I asked him about heaven in the Mormon faith and to paraphrase his reply: the Mormon believers get to meet their boss, but black people cannot. They can look, but not meet. My next thought was: How could anyone possibly believe this?

A close connection people associate with religion is a supposed place in heavenly eternity after death and the comfort faith will provide those left behind. I suppose there are some who get strength from their religion and say they are going to a better world or a better life. How good would it be if they could come back and tell us? A billion years without says that is pretty unlikely.

In that regard, I have a signed last will and testament to make sure there will be no funeral after my death. Normal tradition dictates there's death, there's mourning and there's a funeral. The funeral is like regurgitating the mourning. People will say it is therapeutic, healing, getting on with life and celebrating the life. I don't want any of that. Just pretend I'm still hanging around somewhere. Nor am I in denial about dying. I lost my fear of death playing football. I went into a ruck contest and got knocked out. There was no pain, nothing. I was gone until I woke up in hospital. So if that's death, I'm not worried about it. It's just the shutting off of the brain.

The absence of religion from my life has certainly had no adverse effect or impact on me or my family, or at least none that I am aware of. That said, I have been known to invoke the name of the *Basketball God* from time to time, believing perhaps there is a higher power that uses his or her hand here or there, when situations and outcomes of games are hard to explain or understand.

Having never looked to the supposedly true God – and take your pick from which religion – I now look back and wonder what prompted me to raise the topic of faith as we prepared for the opening match of the 1984 Olympic Games against Brazil. After beating Brazil at the 1972 Olympics and 1982 world championship, Australia had developed a strong rivalry with the South Americans. Coming into the LA Games, we figured Brazil would be a strong team, so victory in the opening match would be crucial for both countries. After going over our strategies and assignments during the pre-game preparation, some kind of instinct took over as I told the players: 'Whatever gods you might pray to – whether it be Jesus, Mary, Muhammad, Confucius, Buddha, Brigham Young or anyone else – do it now because we're going to need all the help we can get.'

In truth, we should have been praying much more when we attended the 1982 world championship in Colombia. Of all the countries I have visited, Colombia is clearly near, or at, the bottom of the pile. It was simply not a nice place to be in. Ever since the mid-1960s, Colombia had been involved in civil conflict with paramilitary and guerrilla groups trying to seize control of the country, corruption was rife, and the drug cartels ruled the streets and the cities without conscience. I would venture to suggest everyone with the Australian team for the tournament was happy to get in, get out and get home. However, Colombia did provide Australia's best effort at a world championship when we finished fifth.

After considering my future at Moscow in 1980, I decided to continue as coach for another Olympic cycle. The emergence of Phil Smyth, Larry Sengstock, Mel Dalgleish and Ian Davies at Moscow provided a strong base for the national team going forward, but more talent and fresh legs were needed. Along with

Smyth, Sengstock, Dalgleish and Davies, Les Riddle and Steve Breheny kept their places for the 1982 world championship. But we went young with six new players: Wayne Carroll, Robert Scrigni, Damian Keogh, Brad Dalton, Ray Borner and Mark Gaze – my nephew and Tony's son. It might have looked like a team for the future, but it produced immediate results in Colombia.

A 75-73 win over Brazil opened the tournament in spectacular fashion before the Soviet Union brought us back down with a heavy defeat. A regulation win over Cote d'Ivoire left us second in Group B to advance to the second phase and a shot at the medal round. The top four teams from the second-round standings would advance to the medal games and we were going well with wins over Canada and Colombia either side of a loss to Spain.

Reality intervened as we were beaten by Yugoslavia and the United States, leaving us fifth with a 4-4 record from a tournament that included Ian Davies finishing second in scoring with 23.4 points per game, a young Doc Rivers running the point for the US, a 17-year-old Arvydas Sabonis on the bench for the USSR, and Oscar Schmidt, a Brazilian scoring machine Australia would face at Los Angeles in 1984 and many times after.

In fact, Australia got to face Oscar and Brazil in the first game of the LA Olympics after the usual detours and hurdles – and meetings with characters – in our long and winding preparation. Needing to qualify for LA from Oceania, Australia swept the series, 2-0, but New Zealand was a tough opponent and we needed to be wary for all 80 minutes. The preparation for the national team through 1983 was not ideal. Fortunately, we were engaged in a three-game series against the touring National Invitation

Tournament All-Stars, a collection of US college players, and that gave us a real workout amid some history and controversy.

After splitting the first two games, we moved to Melbourne for the decider and the very first game to be played at Melbourne Sports and Entertainment Centre, previously the swimming pool for the 1956 Olympics, and soon to become known to all as The Glasshouse. The government spent about $10 million to rejuvenate the venue, refurbishing the seating and laying a basketball court over the pool. It was to be home to Melbourne's NBL teams for the best part of a decade. Unfortunately, it was not the home for basketball we had all hoped for. Regardless, it was a big occasion for basketball in Victoria and the contest and the conclusion lived up to the hype and expectation.

With the scores tied and only seconds remaining, the NIT All-Stars had the ball, but Australia forced a defensive stop and rushed the ball down the floor for a shot at the buzzer. History shows the shot went in for an Australian win. The home team and fans erupted as the basket was made, and all agreed the ball left the shooter's hand before the buzzer. Just as vehemently, the NIT All-Stars argued the ball left the shooter's hand after the buzzer, meaning the basket would be cancelled and we would play overtime. The referees signalled the basket as good and that was when pandemonium and tempers broke loose.

At the end of a buzzer-beating win, rule No.1 is to get your team off the floor and into the locker room as quickly as you can. It is much harder for the officials to change their minds and get the team back on the floor than it is if the players are just standing around. At least that was the theory in the days before instant replay was available. I instructed our players to leave the floor immediately. The referees, perhaps sensing some visiting hostility coming their way, followed the players' lead and scurried for the sanctuary of their locker room. The only problem for them was they were being chased by one of the NIT players, Jim Foster, who was not asking for a calm, rational explanation of the decision. Just as the referees shut and bolted the door behind them, Foster was on the other side, hammering the door and screaming abuse. If the referees had not left the Glasshouse until daybreak, I would not have blamed them.

Having made an impression on the referees, Foster had also made an impression on others. A powerful forward who had played his college ball at South Carolina, Foster signed with Coburg Giants for the 1986 NBL season and showed his talent, averaging 32.2 points per game and 11.0 rebounds. That was good enough for Foster to be named in the All-NBL First team with Steve Carfino, Andrew Gaze, Leroy Loggins and Mark Davis. Pretty good company.

Even with all that talent, the lasting legend of Jim Foster was made off the court and in much more infamous fashion. It has been alleged, possibly among numerous misdeeds, Foster hired a car in Tasmania, put it on the ferry across Bass Strait and sold it in Melbourne. When in Sydney and visiting Kings then-owner Mike Wrublewski at his office, Foster took a light-fingered approach to someone's credit card and became hard to find around the Harbour City. In fact, the whisper around the NBL was Foster could not return to the US because of outstanding warrants for his arrest, hence there were more reported sightings of Foster around Australia and parts of Asia than there were of Elvis around Memphis.

At the end of 1983, the national team toured Canada and the United States West Coast with the aim of preparing for the Los Angeles Olympics. Part of the process involved trying to assess the players considered to be on the fringe of selection. The tour was mixed in terms of results and performances and was probably summed up a little by the game against the University of California-Irvine. We lost despite having probably our best performance of the tour.

Along the way, we were supported, helped and advised by Paul Westhead, whose coaching resume includes the LA Lakers, Chicago Bulls, Denver Nuggets and his legendary high-scoring college team at Loyola-Marymount; former Lakers guard Gail Goodrich, whose knowledge of the game was immense; and Stu Inman, my long-time friend and NBA front office executive, then with the Portland Trail Blazers. In fact, Stu's involvement in our preparation was quite important the closer we got to LA.

There was the growing likelihood of a tit-for-tat Olympic boycott led by the Soviet Union after the US-led boycott of Moscow four years earlier. Bobby Knight, the coach of the US men's Olympic team had led his own boycott, telling college and NBA teams they were not to play or assist foreign teams preparing for LA once they arrived in the US for the Games.

One of the savviest basketball brains and operators in NBA history, Stu found a backdoor route for Australia. Knowing he would cop heat if he defied Knight's edict, Stu rounded up a group of former NBA players and semi-professionals for three games against us in the last 10 days before the Olympic tournament. Keep in mind that only about six weeks earlier, Stu had been front and centre at the NBA draft with the Blazers, taking Sam Bowie with the No.2 pick before the Chicago Bulls chose Michael Jordan at No.3. Stu's time was precious, but his help and input were important and invaluable.

During his schedule, which involved a pre-tournament role with the US, Stu was able to observe a couple of Australian training sessions and games. Given his ability to assess talent, I asked Stu to offer some comments to each of our players, hoping it would provide an edge when we and the individuals needed it most. From his opening comments, I wondered if this plan had backfired. Locking Andy Campbell in his sights, Stu told our biggest big man that, if he was in charge, he would have sent him back to Australia, citing a poor work ethic and lack of commitment. But Stu just as quickly balanced the criticism with some positive comments for Andy to consider, perhaps providing just the right level of wake-up call required. Then Stu went around each of the 11 other players, offering assessments and leaving young Andrew Gaze quite nervous about the impending comments coming his way. I watched and listened in silence and agreed with every comment passed by Stu, even if I might have delivered them in a slightly different manner.

We took the chance to rest for the last couple of days before the Olympic tournament started, especially as I was concerned the players looked fatigued and listless. When I had felt this way as a player at a tournament, I saw the team doctor and received a vitamin B shot, providing instant and dramatic improvement. I suggested the players see the team doctor for a quick check-up and a jab if needed. It wasn't until well after the Olympics I learned most of the players had seen the doctor and received just the boost they needed for the opening game against Brazil and Oscar Schmidt.

An interesting aspect of our team for LA was that only Andrew Gaze and Mark Dalton had not represented Australia at a major international event. They were joined by eight players from the 1982 world championship team - Damian Keogh, Phil Smyth, Larry Sengstock, Wayne Carroll, Mel Dalgleish, Ian Davies, Brad Dalton and Ray Borner – while Andy Campbell and Danny Morseu returned after playing at Moscow in 1980. We felt it was a pretty good team in a tough group with Brazil, Yugoslavia, Germany, Italy and Egypt. We had identified Brazil as the key opponent in the group and that was why, on instinct, I told our players to pray to their god of choice as we headed out to face the South American champion at the Forum.

We trailed by four points at half-time and Ray Borner had put us in a bind by picking up his fourth foul just before the buzzer. Normally, I would have taken him out after his third foul, but we desperately needed his size and strength. It was not Ray's smartest moment, but he was a fast learner and was on his way to becoming one of Australia's most enduring and all-time great players. With Ray in foul trouble, there was gold-plated importance on Larry Sengstock's defensive task against Oscar. Locked-in on that job, Larry kept Oscar to just 14 points, which was outstanding given he finished the Olympics as leading scorer with 24.1 points per game.

On the offensive end, we opted to run the shot clock down as far as we could before getting a good shot away. The theory was to wear down the Brazilians with our ball and player movement and keep the game close with minimal possessions. The only problem with that theory was Brazil defended well and we could not get good high-percentage shots at the end of the offence. Fortunately, the basketball god answered a few prayers as Phil Smyth, Ian Davies and Andrew Gaze connected on some seriously long shots to get us in front and keep us there. The four-point win was a major triumph of perseverance, courage and phenomenal shooting under pressure as Australia started to gain a reputation as the undersized overachievers.

While many were impressed and celebrated our long-range shooting, one man was not, and he accosted me post-game. 'You are a disgrace,' he started off. 'You should never be coaching the game and you should be ashamed of yourself.' I calmly asked what his problem was, and he didn't need asking twice. 'I'm a high school coach and try to teach my players discipline, teamwork and sensible shot selection. You allowed your players to do just the opposite. The shots they took in that game were just outrageous. How can we be expected to teach our players when you are allowing your players to shoot from ridiculous distances like they were today?' I tried to explain our strategy to him and that those shots are fairly standard for Andrew, Ian and Phil, even though the pressure was a bit higher. I'm not sure the high school coach was convinced, and I didn't really care.

On the way out of the venue that day, a security guard mentioned in a friendly, congratulatory way, 'God is an Australian today'. It was an ironic statement given my pre-game suggestion to the players. But if God was Australian that day, I didn't mind admitting His possible existence.

The euphoria of victory quickly gave way to the disappointment of defeat with a 30-point loss to Yugoslavia, certainly a major medal favourite with the Soviet Union staying home. That made the next game against West Germany crucial for our chances of reaching the medal round, but it would not be easy, even though the Germans were the replacement team after the USSR's withdrawal. As always, the Germans were tall and talented with three players – Detlef Schrempf, Christian Welp and Uwe Blab – who were to become NBA first-round draft picks. At 6'10" Schrempf could play either of the forward spots and was a year away from being the eighth pick in the draft; Blab was 7'2" and would go nine places behind Schrempf in the draft; and Welp was a seven-footer playing with Schrempf at the University of Washington and the 16th selection in the 1987 draft. It was a tall order for Australia in more ways than one.

Given our bigs would be stretched by Blab, Welp and others, we opted to use Wayne Carroll on Schrempf. Always looking to post-up smaller opponents and work close to the basket, Schrempf had a five-inch advantage on Wayne, so it was a gamble. It was a gamble that paid off as Wayne had what might have been his finest game in international basketball. After hitting an ominous 30 points in West Germany's opening game against Yugoslavia, Schrempf had 19 against Australia, playing all 40 minutes as Wayne countered with 10 points, seven rebounds, five assists and some excellent defence before fouling out. The efforts of Ray Borner also helped neutralise Welp and the game basically came down to us trying to hold the lead and the Germans trying to force overtime.

The West Germans were sent to the foul line for two free-throws with seconds remaining, needing to make both to force an extra five minutes. I said to assistant coach Adrian Hurley, 'Now we'll see if this guy can handle pressure'. My query was answered resoundingly as the first free-throw hit nothing but net. But my prayers were answered when he clanked the second, we gathered the rebound and held on to win. So often in those situations even the purest shooters develop a steel elbow. Everything about his pre-shot routine and technique was exactly the same for both shots. But halfway through the second, he jerked slightly as if needing to make a correction. Nothing a few squirts of WD40 wouldn't fix.

Tied at halftime of our next game against Italy, Phil Smyth battled manfully against their guards, but we could not shut down Antonello Riva and we lost to the European champion by 11. We were expected to breeze past Egypt in our closing Group A game, but it was much harder than just turning up. After leading by only one at halftime we put on 56 points in the second half to win and finish third in our pool to qualify for a quarterfinal against Spain.

Over the years, our growing rivalries with Brazil and Italy had produced mixed results and performances. Against Spain, the rivalry was lopsided. Quite simply, Spain had always had the better of Australia, and after the Soviet boycott, was essentially the No.1-ranked European team at LA. Led by small forward Juan San Epifanio – known simply as Epi – and power forward/centre Fernando Martin – the first Spaniard to play in the NBA and who tragically died at the age of 27 – Spain was quite a formidable team. But our own efforts in LA meant we were not overawed.

Even though we felt we had closed the gap two years earlier at the world championship in Colombia, we were now quietly confident going into the game as underdogs, that we could finally beat Spain and have a shot at the medals.

It turned out to be a contest of extraordinary offence as Spain shot 37-59 (62.7 per cent) from the field, and Australia went 41-70 (58.6 per cent) and we shared a combined 194 points. Unfortunately, after trailing by seven at halftime, we could only trade baskets in the second half as Epi and Martin totally lived up to their reputations, hitting 50 points between them. Losing teams can always offer excuses rather than reasons for the result. In our case, there were a couple of tough referees' decisions that went against us when we had closed the gap enough to think we could get over the top. We pushed Spain all the way and the relief on their bench, after winning 101-93, was palpable. At the buzzer, Spain coach Antonio Diaz almost dashed across to me, wearing the look of a man who knew he had endured a close call while hugging me in apology and comfort. We were incredibly disappointed by the result after such a good performance, but there was probably some solace down the line when Spain claimed the silver medal. In fact, the United States was the only team to score more against Spain than Australia at the LA Olympics. After posting 101 points in group play, the US scored 96 in the gold medal game.

While Spain went on to play for gold and settled for silver, we went into the crossover rounds for places five to eight and a game against Uruguay. Since winning Olympic silver medals in 1952 and 1956, Uruguay had struggled to even qualify for major events, but had beaten France, Canada and China in LA before losing to Yugoslavia in the quarterfinals. The Uruguayan style of rugged, aggressive basketball – likely to spark physical confrontations – had never appealed to me, and this game was no exception. Our big men did not back down once, but after leading by one at halftime, and scoring 54 in the second half, our shooting touch deserted us down the stretch and we lost by six, 101-95.

As so often was the case, it was now a test of character to see if Australia could quickly regroup and perform after a major disappointment. The strength of character is measured when facing opponents and situations against the odds. That was certainly the case as we prepared to face West Germany for the second time at the LA Games, now to see who finished seventh and eighth. Even though we had beaten the Germans in group play, few outside our squad believed we could repeat the result.

Rather than repeat our defensive tactic from earlier in the tournament, we opted for a match-up zone, aiming to mainly counter Detlef Schrempf. The defensive scheme worked to some degree. We were pounded in the rebounding, but the Germans committed 28 turnovers as Schrempf scored just 14 points on 4-12 shooting. At the other end, Phil Smyth was superb with 22 points on 10-14 shooting as we won, 83-78 to finish seventh. Having gone to LA aiming to win a medal, seventh was disappointing, although marginally satisfying as Australia's best Olympic finish to that point.

After skipping the Moscow Games, the United States returned to Olympic basketball in a big way. Coached by the combustible and controversial Bob Knight, the US ran the table on the way to gold with a team that might have been the best before the Dream Team was assembled for Barcelona in 1992. Such was the desire for Knight to win and to have the right players for his style, future Hall of Famers Charles Barkley and John Stockton were among the players to miss selection. On the team were future NBA stars Patrick Ewing, Chris Mullin, Sam Perkins, Wayman Tisdale, and a guy named Michael Jordan. The LA Olympics were Jordan's global coming-out as a basketballer, making some spectacular and athletic plays, but even that was a mere sample of what was to come with the Chicago Bulls.

With professionalism and commercialism starting to encroach and take over sport in a major way, the LA Games became known as the *Coca Cola Olympics*. The Americans certainly did put their own spin on things, as only they can. But even the pervasive commercialism still seemed to be trailing religion in the battle for signage and patrons. Any time our bus took us along West Jefferson Boulevard, I tried to count the signs that called people to worship and the buildings that had been converted to churches. There were too many to keep an accurate tally and it seemed there were signs and houses-cum-churches every couple of blocks along 10 kilometres of road. There were places with names like the *Church of Last Redemption, Holy Church of Last Hope* and the *Church of Salvation*. The indications were that people needed saving and there were people prepared to save them. I just wondered how many people were in the various congregations and if the donation plates were ever filled. Either way, religion was lost on me. I'd rather go swimming.

POLITICS AND PROS

Coaching was always only a part of what I did in basketball. Aside from looking after Albert Park Stadium and running the Victorian Basketball Association as general manager, I was a delegate to represent Victoria at meetings of the Australian Basketball Federation. Ken Watson was the other Victorian delegate and we always knew we would be fighting losing battles at the ABF board table. While Ken and I were forward-thinking and aimed for the progress of basketball around the country, jealousy and politics usually intervened. It was quite clear at those meetings that, when it came time to vote on proposals, Victoria might have been a basketball power on the court, but the other states often took a chance to have a win at the board table.

The strategy for our opponents was really an open book, and long-serving administrator Ken Madsen once told Ken and I, 'You come to these meetings and are very articulate and erudite with your presentations and you offer very strong and robust debates. But what you never seem to realise is that we had already made a decision on your proposals in the pub the night before'. It was petty politicking that Canberra might not have been able to match.

Given every Victorian proposal took about four years to get passed, Ken and I found a *Trojan horse*. If we had a proposal that we felt needed immediate acceptance, we would persuade a representative from another state to lodge the motion. Usually we would get George Russell from Tasmania to be our ghost proposer and eventually we started winning more than we were losing, at least at the ABF board table.

The opposition to Victoria from the other states actually went deeper than just being an axe to grind with the state body. There was the added element that Ken and I were from Melbourne Tigers and our on-court success and the initiatives we showed as a club – such as touring overseas, tapping into the minds of leading US coaches and hosting clubs and colleges from abroad – was not really celebrated or embraced by too many outside our immediate club circle.

As well as being strong and successful at VBA level, the Tigers had been at the coalface of creating the South East Conference during the 1960s and we dominated the competition for teams from Victoria, South Australia and New South Wales. Unfortunately, the SEC was disbanded after six years because of financial strain on the clubs, but the Australian Club Championship became a surrogate replacement during the 1970s, bringing together the best teams from around the country for a week-long tournament. As expected, the ACC was dominated by Victorian teams with the Tigers and St Kilda Saints sharing most of the titles.

There was also, I believed, a personal issue that some administrators had with me as coach of the Tigers and the Australian men's team. I was accused of recruiting - or not resisting movement of – players from interstate to Victoria. It was claimed that unless you were playing in Victoria you only had a minimal chance of being selected on the national team. It was a rubbish claim, and the best players only ever came to Victoria to play in the best competition. That only made the VBA Championship even stronger.

In reality, South Australia was the only other state with a strong club competition. Nevertheless, the amateurs running basketball in the other states and at national level decided it was someone else's fault rather than doing something to build and improve the standard of play in their own competitions.

Given all that, there was a price to pay. That price – or act of revenge if you prefer that term – came with the formation of the National Basketball League in 1978 with the first season to be played in 1979. Despite being one of the best and strongest teams in Australia, the Tigers were frozen out of the formation and the first five seasons of the NBL.

Not surprisingly, a clandestine movement brought about the NBL. Legend has it the first meeting to form the new competition was held in an aircraft hangar at Sydney Airport. Among those at the meeting were Bruce Johnstone, the pseudo owner of the St Kilda Saints; former national team player and coach John Raschke; and Bob Staunton, who was ABF secretary and wanted the governing body to have some control over the proposed competition. But those pushing the new competition wanted independence and named it the National Invitational Basketball League to lessen ABF oversight.

The early years of the NBL were fraught with problems as it started out trying to balance the number of teams across the country. The 10 teams for the inaugural season were Bankstown Bruins, Brisbane Bullets, Canberra Cannons, City of Sydney Astronauts, Glenelg Tigers, Illawarra Hawks, Newcastle Falcons, Nunawading Spectres, St Kilda Saints and West Adelaide Bearcats. It might have looked good in terms of geographical balance, but in terms of competitive balance, it was disproportionate. Victoria was easily the most dominant state with the best teams but got just two spots in the new league. The political clout at the table gained four places for teams from New South Wales, a lopsided decision if ever there was one. To underline that, St Kilda won the title – beating Canberra in the grand final – and Nunawading was third, tied on the same win-loss record as the Cannons. The four NSW teams filled places six to nine on the ladder with only Glenelg below them. Between them, St Kilda and Nunawading won 28 regular-season games as the four NSW teams combined for 24 victories.

The NBL expanded to 12 teams in 1980, finding a place for the Coburg Giants after they won the ACC, and St Kilda won back-to-back titles. The Saints finished top of the ladder again in 1981 and could have had a hat-trick of NBL titles but opted to skip the playoffs for a trip to Brazil and an unofficial world club championship. It was somewhat disrespectful to blow off the NBL finals – and it was a pity a compromise could not be found – but it also showed the league still had a long way to go to gain the standing it probably deserved and needed.

Either way, there was still no place in the NBL for the Tigers until 1984, earning our way in after winning the South East Basketball League – a reincarnation of the old SEC (later named, Continental Basketball Association, then the South East Australian Basketball League, and most recently NBL1). Winning the SEBL title had become a means of promotion to the NBL, achieved by Geelong and Frankston before us. After biding our time, the Tigers wanted and deserved a place in the NBL, but we found ourselves in something of a transitional period as we prepared for our debut season.

With Brian Goorjian and Al Westover heading into their 30s, both were looking to get into coaching rather than keep playing. Fortunately, we were able to convince them to play at least one NBL season, and it proved crucial given we had a young team aside from them, Olympian Peter Walsh and American Russ Dyer. After that, it was basically a collection of players who had graduated through the Tigers junior program. Among them were Andrew Gaze, Nigel Purchase and Ray Gordon, who would go on to play almost 1300 NBL games between them.

In fact, without the veterans, the Tigers might have been the youngest team in the league. The fact that Al and Brian both stuck around was credit to them, especially because we were essentially asking them to do us a favour. We had no money to speak of so we could not offer cash incentives. All we could do was push the angle that they should play at the top level for as long as they could. Fortunately, they agreed, and I was pleased and proud of the fact Brian and Al – and many others – had a passion for the game and never complained about not being financially rewarded. Importantly, they helped us put together a fairly satisfactory first season in the NBL, finishing with an 11-13 record to be ninth of 17 teams and miss the playoffs by just two wins. While Andrew Gaze led the scoring with 29.1 points per game, Brian was excellent with 21.9 points and 7.5 assists, Al was super consistent with 14.0 points, and Russ Dyer showed his quality with 23.3 points per game.

Even though they only played one NBL season for the Tigers, Brian and Al – and their great mate Bruce Palmer – have a strong place in the hearts and history of the club. Together, all three have an amazing connection to each other, the Tigers and the sport, devoting their lives to coaching after their playing retirements. But, quite possibly, if one had not come to Australia in the 1970s, none of them would have.

The first of the three to come to Melbourne was Brian. I got a call from Bud Pressley, an American college coach I had become friendly with. Bud said he had a player I might be interested in signing. Bud knew Brian's dad, Ed, who was a top high-school coach in California. Brian had finished his four years at Pepperdine University, so Bud thought Australian basketball would be a good opportunity. That recommendation was enough for me, because knowing Bud, he did not hand out favours easily.

As a coach, Bud was infamously demanding, especially on defence, to the point of being fanatical. In fact, one story goes that Bud was running a drill where his players had to stand in front of a driving player and take a charge. Infuriated that the players were not putting their bodies on the line, Bud demanded they stand aside, and he got in a defensive stance to confront the driver. The coach took the charge right in the middle of the chest. Which was good, except for the fact Bud had recently undergone heart bypass surgery and the contact from the charge had re-opened his wound. Such was Bud's notorious intensity that his wife lived in a separate house during the basketball season. Bud also taught and demanded a possession-based motion offence because, 'No snot-ty-nosed kid is going to make me lose my job'.

With Bud's recommendation, Brian arrived in Australia and we set about reprogramming him as a basketball player.

Throughout his high school and college careers, Brian had never had to set a screen and never had to come off a screen. His job had been to pass the ball and hit the perimeter shot. But with the Tigers' Shuffle offence, there was plenty of screening and cutting that Brian had to learn and get used to. It took some time, but he got there, and he did so in his own fashion, which I called *Brian Goorjian Syndrome*: when he had the ball, the play was going to finish in two possible ways: Brian shooting, or the player he passed to shooting it. With some freedom within our structure, Brian was a very good player.

Having experienced how good life was in Australia, Brian said he had a mate who was keen to come out. That mate was Bruce Palmer. Again, Brian's word was good enough for me, so we brought Bruce to Melbourne. There was a real competitive edge to Bruce, who had played at the University of the Pacific, and he had an inherent resistance to authority. Hence, Bruce never really got on well with referees or officialdom. Blessed with copious amounts of sarcasm and charm, there was a 50-50 chance Bruce would greet an official with a friendly handshake or just get things out of the way and tell him to kiss his bum.

So, it was something of a gamble when, in my role as VBA general manager, I appointed Bruce as referee director. It could have been like flicking a flame into a dry wheat field given Bruce was notorious for baiting referees and getting into disputes with officials. It turned out the exact opposite. Bruce was a strong advocate for the referees and a great motivator. The referees were disappointed when he left that role and became a champion-ship-winning coach.

On the court in our offence, Bruce was the cutter and Brian was the feeder, so they connected throughout the game. But the connection off the court was better entertainment than anything they were showing on television. When Bruce and Brian were together they were – and still are – a formidable comedy duo with storytelling and repartee that makes a two-hour drive from Newcastle to Sydney on a road trip seem like five minutes.

Soon enough, Bruce recommended his college teammate, Al Westover. No problem. When Al arrived, he played with our second team, Auburn Tigers, in the VBA and then moved to the Melbourne roster when an import spot opened up. It wasn't quite *The Three Stooges*, but it was three outstanding basketball men and Al eventually had the longest association with the Tigers, circling back to be my assistant coach after he played with Geelong Supercats, went to Dandenong Rangers as player-coach, and then Ballarat Miners as head coach. Aside from being an excellent assistant with the NBL team, Al also coached the Tigers juniors and helped develop some top players over the years.

It was only fitting and right that when I stepped down at the end of the 2005 NBL season, that Al moved one seat up the bench to become head coach of the Tigers. Undaunted and 100 per cent ready, Al led the Tigers to the NBL title in his first season as head coach and won a second championship in 2008. In fact, Al had the impressive record of taking the Tigers to four NBL grand finals in his first four seasons as coach. It was incredibly disappointing when Al was sacked in the middle of the 2010-11 season. I thought it was unjustified, but that's what happens when you're not in charge of your own destiny. When it comes to coaches and people, Al is one of the good ones with a great personality and incredible loyalty.

Interestingly, Al was the last out of he, Brian and Bruce to coach in the NBL. After coaching Ballarat Miners, Brian was hired by Eastside Melbourne Spectres (previously Nunawading), and Bruce joined North Melbourne Giants (previously Coburg) after he had coached Coburg women and Dandenong Rangers men. Al actually followed Brian at Ballarat and led the Miners to success before he moved back to Melbourne and the Tigers. All three won NBL titles – Brian topping the all-time list with six: two with South East Melbourne Magic, three with Sydney Kings and one with South Dragons.

Any kind of success was a long time coming for Melbourne Tigers in the NBL. After a promising first season, it was a battle from year to year and those early years had an element of rebuilding about it for us. While we had good young players, our lack of financial strength meant we were well behind every other NBL team when it came to trying to sign big names or paying any player any kind of meaningful money. We were still pretty much an amateur club in most senses while others were becoming more professional. Fortunately, good luck and good timing coincided to present good opportunity.

One night as I was coaching one of the Tigers junior teams, a man approached me out of the blue and asked what it would take to be successful in the NBL. My immediate response was that we needed a good board. Every good club needs an influential board to oversee operations and governance. He said simply, 'I think I can help you with that'. It turned out the enquiring gent was the head of the Victorian Treasury, and he was a mate of the Treasurer. There were other government colleagues keen to get on board and soon enough it seemed we could hold State Government Cabinet meetings at Tigers games. These men of influence were able to introduce us to the key sponsors who were able to provide the financial support we needed to make an impact on the floor. It was nice to have the big end of town on our side.

The development of our board, sponsorship and financial structure eventually helped us improve on the court and it came at a time when the Melbourne NBL teams were looking at moving into better facilities. The Giants, Saints and Spectres all moved to the Glasshouse, and the Tigers eventually left Albert Park to join them. The NBL was catching the attention of fans, media and sponsors and the game was on the move. It was logical to move into a bigger and better venue. While I liked the Glasshouse, I felt it was somewhat awkward that the tight seating arrangement in the stands meant your knees were either side of the head of the person sitting in front of you.

As the NBL continued to grow, there was a push to leave the Glasshouse and play games at Rod Laver Arena – or Melbourne Park as it was then known – in the early 1990s. The Tigers led the move and the others followed, but the inevitable economic dangers that fledgling professional sporting teams and organisations endure came to the fore. Quite simply, the venue operators – in this case Melbourne and Olympic Park Trust – were the only ones making any kind of money on the deal. At the Glasshouse, we could manage with smaller crowds. Once we crossed Swan Street, we could never get ahead financially, even when we eventually left

Rod Laver for the new and smaller venue now named Melbourne Arena. It simply became an exercise in the MOPT making money and the NBL teams going into financial cardiac arrest.

Some of the accounting just seemed ridiculous. An excellent example was one weekend when we had a home game with about 6000 people in attendance. That was around the break-even point and we got a cheque for $650 from MOTP. The following weekend we had a crowd close to 7000 and we received less money. I asked venue management about this anomaly and wanted an explanation. After checking, the manager said there had been extra set-up costs because there had been an event the night before our game. My response was not printable. We had a walk-in walk-out arrangement, but we were charged for an event that had nothing to do with us. That was just one example of how difficult it was to get ahead in those venues. The fact the government said it would make Melbourne Arena a dedicated basketball facility and then basically built a cycling velodrome tells you everything you need to know.

That said, during the early to mid-90s when we filled Rod Laver Arena, it was like nothing else. I remember walking from the dressing room to the court before one of our grand final games against South East Melbourne Magic. As I emerged to see the crowd of 15,000, it was a life experience coming to fruition. Not just for me, but for a lot of people. To see that venue packed provided a sense of achievement and satisfaction that had been many, many years in the making.

Coming off the 1984 NBL season, that kind of ambition was still considered worthy of admittance to the psychiatric ward of the nearest hospital. Even more so over the next four seasons as the Tigers competed without posting too many wins. After that promising debut season, we went 5-21, 6-20, 3-23 and 8-16. It was a struggle to say the least, but by 1989 our new board structure and improving finances helped push us into the NBL playoffs for the first time, going 16-8 over the regular season.

While we still had a solid, honest core of younger players who were now maturing, there were two players who lifted us to the next level: David Simmons and David Colbert. An undersized centre in college, Dave Colbert was a beast from anywhere on the floor for the Tigers, and Dave Simmons was a force inside the paint. During a US tour at the end of the 1988 season, we were put in contact with Dave Simmons as a potential recruit, so we asked for a scrimmage to be organised to see how he looked. When Andrew Gaze and I arrived at the gym, there was only Dave and another guy there. Everyone else was a no-show. So, Andrew and I played Dave and the other guy two-on-two. It was enough for us to see that he would be OK. When Dave finished the 1989 season with 26.3 points per game and 9.9 rebounds, we all thought he was a bit better than OK. It was the same with Dave Colbert, who had 25.8 points and 11.8 rebounds.

The first experience of the playoffs finished in the first round for the Tigers, beaten by the Sydney Kings 2-1 in the best-of-three format. But the season was a major turning point for the club as the two Daves committed their futures to the program. Dave Colbert, who died at the young age of 47, spent three seasons with the Tigers, and Dave Simmons was with us for eight years, becoming a club legend with his No.25 retired to the rafters.

As much as helping us on the court, Dave Colbert and Dave Simmons helped usher in the truly professional era of the Tigers. From the days of relying on Americans to move to Australia to work as schoolteachers, or to basically come out on the promise of nothing more than a chance to play basketball and work a 9-to-5 job, we were in a position where we could actually pay players a decent wage.

Either way, nothing changed for me financially. I had never been paid to play or coach. When we moved into the NBL and money started becoming a factor, the board wanted me to be paid. I told them I would accept some payment when the club could afford it. I had always been an amateur and the issue of being paid was not one I ever wrestled with. I was handsomely paid with great experiences and the satisfaction of competition. The game had gone pro, but I hadn't.

WINNING TIME

The periods of euphoria or despair I experienced during my career as a player and coach were always very brief. As a player, we would win the Victorian Basketball Association Championship on Wednesday night, and on Thursday morning I would be on the court at Albert Park, shooting and trying to correct any errors or faults I might have encountered 12 hours earlier. As a coach, it was the same. Up early the next morning to get into the office for work while churning over the game in my head to tick off plays or aspects of the 40 minutes that need refining and working on.

It was the same when Melbourne Tigers finally broke through and won their first NBL championship in 1993. There was a quick celebration with those closest to the team and it was onto the next task and challenge. It was the same when we won again in 1997. We played and beat South East Melbourne Magic at Rod Laver Arena and then had a function over the road at the Glasshouse. I was there briefly. I might have done one lap of the room to congratulate and thank the people who helped over the season and then I was gone. That sort of thing was just never my atmosphere. I wasn't tuned into excessive celebration, and I didn't need to exaggerate the experience of winning.

After our initial playoff appearance in 1989, winning became a habit for the Tigers and we eventually became serious contenders for the NBL title. We had to replace Dave Colbert for the 1992 season and were recommended a player with NBA experience. We decided to go with him. By signing Lanard Copeland, we not only got an outstanding basketball player, but a great person and someone who became enshrined in the history of the Melbourne Tigers as one of the club's all-time greats. That said, there were some doubts about Lanard after his first training session with the Tigers.

A late bloomer, Lanard was lucky to get a college scholarship at Georgia State University, not exactly a basketball powerhouse. The story goes a scout spotted Lanard playing pick-up ball and that led to him going to college and eventually to the NBA with the Philadelphia 76ers and Los Angeles Clippers. That Lanard only got on the floor in 33 NBA games was not a reflection of his talent, but more a fact the NBA is very much about being in the right situation at the right time. Either way, there was a lot of expectation that accompanied Lanard to Melbourne and his first training session with the Tigers not too far out from the 1992 season.

As with any new import on any NBL team, the first impression can be important, and Lanard's first impression was awful. Here we had this impressive-looking athlete coming from the NBA and he was taken apart by Dean Vickerman, whose basketball career had taken him as far as the Tigers bench. It was a no-contest and there were a few puzzled looks. In fairness, Lanard had only landed that day. With his legs under him and a decent sleep, he showed he would more than suit our needs, and underlined it in the first game of the season, which also happened to be the Tigers' first game at Melbourne Park. Andrew Gaze was finishing his season in Italy with Udine and missed the game, but when Lanard took the opening tip from Dave Simmons and went to the basket for a dunk, a legend was in the making.

When Andrew got back home, he and Lanard formed an instant bond on and off the court with a basketball partnership and friendship that has endured to this day. They complemented each other as basketball players and formed one of the greatest guard combinations in NBL history. More than that, Australia became home to Lanard and he became a naturalised citizen and father to four beautiful daughters. In fact, the task of retaining quality imports was helped if the player met and fell for a local lady. More often than not, if the import arrived with a wife or girlfriend, there was a good chance she would want to go home long before he did.

Either way, Lanard had only intended to come to Australia for one season before again trying the NBA or heading to Europe. The reason Lanard returned for a second season was to go one step better than his first. After being around the mark for several years, the Tigers made the grand final in 1992 and faced South East Melbourne Magic, coached by Brian Goorjian. As always, the series was a true battle as Darren Lucas locked onto Andrew and never let go, one showing his defensive prowess, the other an amazing ability to score no matter the attention paid.

After finishing third on the ladder at the end of the regular season, we needed three games to beat Perth Wildcats in the quarterfinals, we needed another three games to beat Sydney Kings in the semi-finals, and we took Game 1 of the best-of-three grand final series against the Magic by 18 points. We were one win away from our first NBL title, but the Magic won the next two in a series that drew more than 15,000 people to Melbourne Park for every game. The disappointment was palpable, and it brought

Lanard back in 1993. The Tigers also signed Mark Bradtke from the Adelaide 36ers and, like Lanard, he became a massive part of the club's history and success.

Although we finished the regular season with a 16-10 record, we got going in the playoffs, sweeping the quarters and semis against the Illawarra Hawks and Magic. That set up a best-of-three grand final against the Perth Wildcats. Given Perth had the home court for Games 2 and 3, it was imperative the Tigers won Game 1. We got there by four points, putting the onus on the Wildcats going back to Perth. The series was evened 1-1 when the Wildcats took Game 2 by seven points and there was a genuine sense among the Perth fans that the series was over. They were convinced the Wildcats would win Game 3 on the Sunday and put another championship banner in the rafters. They had this idea the Wildcats could not be beaten in Perth, especially by the Tigers. Without gloating, I'm glad to say they got it wrong.

Our players were locked in and on a mission. One vivid memory is of Andrew Vlahov's shot doing a lap of the rim and coming back out when going in would have given the Wildcats a late and important lead. We regained composure and Andrew Gaze made one free-throw with about four seconds left to seal the win. After hitting 41 points in Game 1, Andrew had 22 in the decider and Mark Bradtke had 22 points and 19 rebounds. Having been hell-bent on avenging the grand final defeat of 12 months earlier, Lanard had 35 points in Game 3 to underline his quality and fulfil his goal.

Perhaps the greatest compliment I could give that Tigers team of 1993 was that it embodied one of sport's oldest adages: a team of champions does not guarantee a champion team. The essential ingredient to any successful team – any championship-winning team – is champion people.

The 1993 team included four undisputed champion players: Andrew Gaze, Lanard Copeland, Dave Simmons and Mark Bradtke. But there would not have been a championship without the contributions of their team-mates. Ray Gordon grew up through the Tigers junior ranks with Andrew Gaze and was considered part of our family. Steven Whitehead, Andrew Walter and Nick Tenner also were graduates of the Tigers juniors. Warrick Giddey's statistics were disproportional to his contribution and importance, and Robert Sibley provided as many intangible benefits as he did tangible.

In fact, Rob was a good example of a what a champion person can give to a team. On the court, Sibley was the type of player you loved to have on your team, but opponents hated to play against. At just on 200cm tall and with a gym freak's physique, he was fiercely loyal, and team orientated. Rather than score, Rob preferred to set lethal screens for team-mates and adopt the role of protector. It was not uncommon for him to be in foul trouble, more often than not because of his dedication to looking after team-mates.

Off the court, Rob was genial and popular with everyone, usually with a large group gravitating to him at our post-game functions. It was at one of those post-game gatherings that I discovered Rob's smoking habit. Noticing a large bulge inside his tight-fitting shirt, closer inspection revealed a tucked-away packet of cigarettes. Knowing I was strongly opposed to smoking, Rob was like a child caught with his hand in the cookie jar. Although not quite apologetic, he promised he would abstain in the future. That said, I think he was proud of the fact he had been able to keep his smoking habit secret from me. Rob was and is a free spirit, fun to be around and a champion person. Just the kind of person every team needs to be successful.

Unfortunately, the 1993 grand final was memorable for more than just winning. It was memorable because it was decided in Perth and the majority of the Wildcats fans served a massive reminder of how not to behave in defeat. From the outset, the Perth fans were absolutely and totally committed to the impossibility they could lose because Games 2 and 3 were in Perth. 'We never lose to Melbourne in Perth,' became their mantra. It turned out to be brainwashing. The Tigers had beaten the Wildcats in Perth, just not at Perth Entertainment Centre. In their early days in the NBL, Perth struggled to beat a drum. But the program had turned around significantly with the money of owner Kerry Stokes and the energy of Cal Bruton as player and coach to the point the Wildcats had won titles in 1990 and 1991. It was a case of the bandwagon fans almost having a sense of entitlement when it came to winning games and titles.

That attitude came to a head at the post-game presentation of the championship trophy. Our players and fans celebrated as expected on the buzzer, but there was nothing outlandish or unsportsmanlike. In fact, the enduring and endearing image of the immediate aftermath is of Andrew putting me in a headlock of unrestrained joy, at least for him. But as Andrew stepped up to receive the trophy, the remaining Wildcats fans erupted into a sustained chorus of boos. That they booed Andrew to silence was an act I have never understood. I have come to understand we were not unique to be on the end of that response, but that never placated me. I thought Andrew deserved more respect than that, pure and simple.

A couple of people from Perth sent me letters apologising for the booing, which I appreciated. But the actions of most of those fans took the edge off winning. What should have been a great moment in Tigers history – and the players' chance to be rightly lauded – was overshadowed by a level of unsportsmanlike behaviour that no individual or team deserved.

As the 1990s moved on, the Wildcats became slightly lesser rivals for the Tigers. The continued emergence of the South East Melbourne Magic provided the Tigers with a challenge on and off the court. The Melbourne rivalry also took the NBL and basketball to another level in Australia with unprecedented interest, attendances and media coverage.

The spike enjoyed by the NBL in the early to mid-1990s has been partly explained as the Michael Jordan Phenomenon. The rise of Jordan with the Chicago Bulls and the appearance of the Dream Team at the 1992 Barcelona Olympics had really opened the NBA to the world. Television coverage of the NBA in Australia was still intermittent, but it seemed every young basketball player wanted to emulate Jordan. Coupled with the rising standard of the NBL, the Jordan Phenomenon helped create a new culture, which brought people to games, and that helped the NBL get to a prominent position in professional Australian sport. By 1996, sell-out crowds of 15,000 at Melbourne Park were not unusual, especially when the Tigers faced the Magic.

After winning the 1993 title, the Tigers took a back seat to the North Melbourne Giants – coached by one of our former assistants, Brett Brown – in 1994, and the Wildcats in 1995. But in 1996, the rivalry between the Tigers and Magic was on in earnest. There was little love lost between the teams as the Magic cultivated a tough-guy *Men in Black* image, and there were often physical clashes and confrontations. Those confrontations provided plenty of spark for the fans and media to start fires. There was also so much talent on both teams that the basketball was of the highest quality.

Over the course of the 1996 season, the Tigers and Magic were clearly the best two teams in the league and seen as coming from opposite directions. The Tigers had an offensive philosophy of scoring points, the Magic had a defensive mindset to lockdown opponents no matter what. Never was that exemplified more than the one-on-one battles between Andrew Gaze and Darren Lucas. Not surprisingly, the Magic identified the need to limit Andrew's scoring and influence, and Darren was single-minded in that role, using whatever means necessary to get the job done. I recall seeing a photo of tip-off for a Tigers-Magic game and on the edge of the circle, Darren already had his arms wrapped around Andrew, pushing the envelope even before the clock had started, daring the referees to make a call. It should be said Darren was never malicious in guarding Andrew, but it would not have been surprising to learn he was right there when Andrew rolled over in his sleep later that night.

Despite our good regular-season, we were given a real wake-up call in the first playoff game, losing to the Bullets in Brisbane by

21. We recovered to take the quarterfinal in the third-and-deciding game, and the semi-final series followed the same pattern, losing to Canberra Cannons before closing it out at home to set-up a best-of-three grand final against the Magic. After taking Game 1, we lost a close Game 2, and then got blown out in Game 3 by 37. The Magic held us to just 70 points in the deciding game and, fittingly, Mike Kelly, a smart basketballer with an amazing commitment to defence, was named grand final Most Valuable Player. After losing by such a large margin there could be no ifs, ands or buts. All we could do was look ahead to 1997. If only it had been that easy.

After 12 games of the 1997 season, the Tigers were 3-9 and things were looking pretty ordinary. In fact, if I had been coaching any other NBL team, I would have been fired for two reasons: our record, and the fact the people who make those decisions don't really know what is happening within the team. In our case, we had a couple of injuries and a bureaucratic problem with Mark Bradtke as he returned to the NBL after a season in the NBA with the Philadelphia 76ers. We also had a couple of close losses, and it was clear to me we had the tools. We knew changes would not happen overnight. We just needed to refine things and maybe have a little luck along the way.

The biggest change we made was to release import forward Jarvis Lang. While Jarvis averaged 19 points and nine rebounds per game, he was struggling with knee problems. After the first six games of the season, Jarvis sat out the next two games. But after two more games with him in the line-up, we were 3-8 and 1-6 in the last seven, and we decided to make a change.

There is never a guarantee of success when signing an import, even with weeks to do research and scouting. It is a significant risk to change imports mid-season. It may have been on the suggestion of Brett Brown that we have a look at Marcus Timmons, who had been in the NBL with the Illawarra Hawks. We signed Marcus and he became a major contributor in a massive turnaround as the Tigers headed for the 1997 championship from a long way back.

Between Jarvis leaving and Marcus arriving, we split a pair of games to be 4-9 on the season. It would be easy to say Marcus was the immediate answer to our problems, but that would be lying. Although we won the first game Marcus played with us, he and the Tigers were inconsistent as we battled to a 6-11 record after an eight-point loss to the Giants. It was to be the last game the Tigers would lose in the regular-season as we put together a 13-game winning streak, scoring almost 110 points per game across that run to finish second on the ladder behind the Magic. An interesting fact that may have eluded most people, at the time and since, was the Tigers actually swept the Magic 3-0 during the regular season. As the playoffs arrived, the Magic may well have been looking over their shoulder.

After a bye in the first round of the playoffs, a sweep of the Giants in the semi-final took the Tigers' winning streak to 15 games. It was a close two-game series with the margins being eight points and seven points, but it was enough for a spot in the best-of-three grand final against the Magic, the third time in six years we had faced each other for the championship. Game 1 was no contest. The Tigers shot at 60 per cent from the field and won 111-74, making it an NBL-record 16 straight wins.

Typically, the Magic made the right adjustments, turned it into a low-scoring battle and took Game 2, 84-78. With only a few days between Games 2 and 3, we reset and went to work. By halftime we led by 14 and were up by 15 after three periods. We won by 10 for a 17th victory in 18 games to claim a second NBL title for the Tigers. Our so-called *Big Four* was superb as Lanard had 26 points in Game 3 and was named grand final MVP, followed by Andrew with 22, Mark Bradtke with 21 and Marcus with 20.

The Philadelphia 76ers recently made some waves with the catchcry 'Trust the process'. The Tigers did just that 20 years earlier. While bringing in Marcus certainly helped us win the title in 1997, it was not the only factor. It was really a matter of faith in the people and the process. The main core of our roster had not really changed since winning the 1993 championship, so it was almost as simple as staying positive through the down periods, knowing one win would lead to two, and two would lead to three and so on.

Every win brings more confidence, and confidence allows us to do things easier. That was what we did. We built on it and by the end of the season we were playing pretty well. There was some anxiety along the way and if we had lost faith in each other, it would have been disastrous. But the experience of the older players was a key to keeping things together. It was not the first time we had been in a hole, and it was not the last, but we knew we had to revisit the basics and stick with them. Patience, togetherness and an emphasis on the positives rather than the negatives were the only way to get to where we wanted to be and where we knew we could go.

Maybe Marcus coming in was a key, especially with his personality. Relaxed and unstressed, Marcus is not a complex character and he fit right in with the team on and off the court. When it comes to Marcus, the Tigers and the Gazes consider him family. Marcus is the kind of guy that when the crap is flying, he will just step forward and, almost disbelieving there might be panic, say, 'Don't worry. I got this'. Which probably happened more than a few times during the 1997 season.

When people mention the 1997 season, they talk of the 16-game winning streak and they talk of the Tigers starting line-up as one of the best – if not the best – to have played in the NBL. We had Andrew Gaze and Lanard Copeland in the guard spots, Warrick Giddey and Marcus Timmons as forwards, and Mark Bradtke at centre. We had four genuine scorers and Wazza, who was one of the best defensive players, passers and teammates any team could ever have. An international rugby player as a schoolboy, Wazza was as tough as he was unselfish, executing the unseen one per cent actions that make such a difference. He also laid a couple of hammers on Mike Kelly and Sam Mackinnon in that 1997 series, going right to the edge without going over.

All I will say on the quality of that five is, I don't know where this group ranks in NBL history, but they were fairly good, and we won. After all, what is the benefit of trying to compare players and teams of one era with those of another? It is that old thing that you can't compare apples and oranges except to say they both taste good. It also comes back to my outlook that yesterday is gone, and tomorrow is a new day. The euphoria of today quickly becomes the joy of yesterday and is replaced by the excitement of what is yet to come. Which was why after we won that 1997 championship, I completed a lap of the room at the post-game celebration, thanked and congratulated as many people as I could and headed home.

It was legendary rugby league coach Jack Gibson who became famous for the line that winning starts Monday. All I knew was that we might have won a championship on Saturday, but I needed to be in the office on Monday, working, planning and looking ahead. Winning never changed that.

LINDA AND MAGGOT

Sitting in my hotel room in Tianjin, there was a knock on the door. On answering, I was handed a box. In the box was plenty of coaching attire: shirts, tracksuit, shoes. I had been in the city for two days and was thankful for the prompt delivery. But one aspect of the package was a little unnerving. Without having been measured or asked to supply sizes, every item fitted perfectly, even the shoes. I asked how this was possible and never really got an answer. Welcome to China and don't ask questions.

Ever since my first visit to China in the 1970s, it has never failed to live up to its reputation as a country of great history along with great intrigue and mystery. So, going back there to coach the Tianjin Gold Lions in 2007 was a great opportunity and an amazing experience, and one that was totally unexpected, born out of a polite throw-away comment.

Melbourne City Council had invited me to a function for a sister city, Tianjin. During the event, I chatted about basketball with some of the Chinese delegation and the fact Tianjin's new team had an ambition to play in the top division of the Chinese Basketball Association. As the conversation wound up, I said, 'If there's anything I can do to help, let me know'. When you say that, 99 per cent of the time nothing happens. This time, the one per cent happened. A phone call two weeks later led to a meeting, which led to an offer to coach the Tianjin Gold Lions.

It was, from memory, my first negotiation to be a coach, and it was not anything outrageous. While there would be a financial element to the deal, one of the important conditions was that I had to have Internet access, not a common thing in China. I needed to be able to still administrate the Melbourne Basketball Association competitions, hence the need for Internet. The men from Tianjin agreed and I signed. In fact, needing the Internet provided some unexpected bonuses. On some road trips, I would be sent to a different hotel than the team. My hotel had Internet access and the accommodation was better quality.

Internet access wasn't the only thing that has changed in the 40-odd years since I had first been to China. It is fair to say the entire country had undergone a massive transformation from a mysterious, archaic backwater ruled by staunch communists and closed to the outside world. China had become a thriving global economic power with a firm grasp and enjoyment of capitalism, technology and Western culture. Basketball was clearly trying to follow a similar path.

The dark veil over China started to lift to the outside world after US President Richard Nixon visited the country in 1972 and met with Chairman Mao Zedong in an effort to re-establish diplomatic relations between the nations. But before that historic meeting had been what became known as Ping Pong Diplomacy, the invitation for the US table tennis team to visit China in 1971. Competitive sport was basically banned in China during Mao's Cultural Revolution. But table tennis and basketball survived the period and came out the other side.

This allowed Australian national teams to visit and play in China during tours of Asia. After table tennis, basketball was a favourite of the Chinese, and to go there in the 1970s was an adventure in more ways than one, both on and off the basketball court. On one tour, we flew into Hong Kong and then took a train to the Chinese border and onto Guangzhou, where we were greeted by many officials and the offer of as many cigarettes as we liked. Just as quickly, it seemed we were at a welcoming function, seated in a VIP area that was separated from the rest of the room by a giant pond filled with golden carp. The 12-course meal included unborn sparrow and pig testicles, and my explanation of being vegetarian allowed me to politely decline the local delicacies. Unfortunately, there was no escaping the shots of White Lightning, a potent local liqueur that was downed after every toast and speech.

There were many toasts and speeches that night, but our touring party survived intact, except for Michael Tucker, who spent the next day in bed. A local doctor administered an injection that seemed to help Michael, who recovered to play in the games against various club teams, which became more physical and aggressive the more we won. With one more game to play, we were given tours of the Emperor's Palace, Tiananmen Square, the Forbidden City, the Ming Tombs and the Great Wall. To cap off those glorious sights was another 12-course banquet. Still a little fatigued, Michael was excused from the farewell dinner after receiving another mystery injection from a Chinese medical man. On hearing this was about to happen, I tried to intervene, but arrived just as the syringe was being wiped on the sleeve of the medicine man's white jacket. Within an hour, *Tuck* had red lines crawling up his arm and the onset of a high fever. Before heading off to the banquet, I stopped to see how *Tuck* was doing. Looking at me with a rueful smile, Michael asked, 'Does everyone have this much fun on their first trip?'

The idea of Chinese medicine as an alternative treatment or therapy is quite accepted now by many Westerners. Stuff like acupuncture and herbal remedies. But in the 1970s and 1980s we were not quite ready for some of the magical remedies, such as how to mend a sprained ankle. One of our players went over hard on his ankle, which would normally mean the end of the game for him. But he was taken to the locker room by our Chinese delegate and soon re-emerged, declaring himself ready to play. We looked at him like he was mad. He told us the Chinese medical man had taken what looked like a teabag, slapped it on the ankle, rubbed in some other potion and the problem was solved. He went back on and played.

But even in the ensuing 30 years, it did not seem like sports medicine in China had kept pace – or even been close – to the progress of sports medicine in the West. As we were ready to start a training session with Tianjin, someone told me one of the players could not take part because he was injured and had just had treatment. But the player attended the session and had marks over his body that looked like leeches had been poured over him and gone to work. Whatever it was, it worked, and he was back on the floor the next day.

An example of China being closed to the outside world also came on that first trip when our interpreter wanted to know the title of the most popular book in Australia at the time. I said it was *The Exorcist*, which was a controversial novel even for the liberal West. He quietly asked if I could get him a copy, which I did, amazingly via the Australian embassy. I gave him the book and, leaving it wrapped in its brown paper bag, he devoured it down the back of the team bus. To be reading this Western propaganda in China was highly risky, but this guy seemed to have a mind of his own. He later travelled to Australia with the Chinese women's team and there is a suspicion he may have defected. But nobody seemed to know for sure. After all, China would not acknowledge if he had defected or if he had been returned to the homeland and an uncertain future.

Touring China was to have your eyes opened and receive a tremendous education. It also served to underline how fortunate we were in Australia and that we should never take our lifestyle and freedom for granted.

In short, the Chinese people in the big cities were oppressed and forced to follow the communist doctrine, and those in the rural areas were peasants eking out an existence in the fields. But the propaganda unit of the government did its best to show that China and its people were united and happy. In every province we visited, there were signs proclaiming that province was a leader in a certain field. The reality was far different.

The workers in factories and on building sites faced the worst and most dangerous conditions. The scaffolding was bamboo poles laced together, and the factory workers did whatever long hours they were told to do. Working past midnight was not unusual.

In the 1970s, it was estimated as much as 80 per cent of China's population – at that stage just short of one billion people – lived in rural areas and worked the land. Inevitably, the people have moved from the country to urban settings. I couldn't imagine how the transfer of so many people from the rural areas to the cities could be managed over a short period of time, but they did, and they have.

Back in the '70s, the Chinese Government was proudly talking up its process of mechanising the farms with modern equipment. But on one bus trip to visit a commune, there was a line of people shoulder-to-shoulder for as far as we could see, digging an irrigation channel along the side of the road. Up to their waists in water, they were creating the channel by scooping the earth out by hand. They didn't even have a shovel between them.

At the commune, the local officials proudly showed us their new medical centre. There were a few looks shared among our group. Imagine a horse stable constructed of concrete with a water trough attached to the wall that doubled as the sterilisation unit. There were bare floors, natural light, rusting dental chairs and so many patients waiting for attention, you had to wonder at the attrition rate, especially if someone had a serious illness. It was positively medieval, but for a commune to have its own medical centre was an achievement and something to be proud of.

As backward as it might have seemed, and as hard as the Chinese had it, you could rarely criticise the people themselves for their spirit and outlook. Like the caretaker of an abandoned temple I met. He was very proud of the temple, even though it was no longer used or needed. He told us the temple had been built to pray for rain to ensure a good harvest. But with better education, they realised that praying for rain doesn't always work. Plus, they now had irrigation. Either way, the caretaker was happy.

The people of China are fascinating, but Western visitors were even more fascinating for the Chinese, especially in the more remote cities. One time while out exploring a city, I was on the street corner waiting for the traffic lights to change and was approached by one of the locals. Without saying a word, he got his face as close to my face as he possibly could. It was like he had stumbled across an alien from Mars and was studying me intently. So, I summoned up my best Mandarin and said, 'Ni hao'. Hello. The man broke into the broadest smile and displayed the shiniest set of stainless-steel teeth I had ever seen. But, again, he was so happy to have such a simple interaction.

On another occasion, I was in the hotel elevator and the only other occupant was a well-dressed, middle-aged woman. She asked me, 'How old are you?' I was surprised by the question and wondered why she asked. I responded, 'I am old. Very old'. She replied, 'Oh, I thought you were younger than that'.

The other aspect of China that always drew me back – and was a factor in accepting the role with Tianjin – was the history and culture. Over the years, I have been fortunate to visit places such as the Forbidden Palace, where the artefacts, jewellery and jade made the UK Royal Family's collection look like a stall at a Sunday market. I admired and was amazed at the intricate craftwork that goes into making ivory pieces. I recall watching a master of his craft working on a small ivory carving of a fishing vessel with a net. I was told it had taken five years to do. The patience, devotion and attention to detail told you something about the Chinese people.

Having learned and experienced the culture of China ensured I went into the coaching role at Tianjin fully versed in the knowledge that an open mind and remaining calm were essential. In China, it is important to know the hierarchy, the system of how things work and who has the ultimate say in what happens. That was a little more complicated in some ways at Tianjin, given the team was one of the last pro outfits managed by the local government.

As with observing the hierarchy, it is important to ensure the Chinese are never embarrassed or humiliated. It is called saving face, and something we grew accustomed to following and dealing with during our games there with the Tigers. It was important the players all knew how things worked. If we were going to win, we could not win by too wide a margin. If the local team held a lead or it looked like we might get too far ahead, expect the refs to make calls against us and do not complain or dispute the calls. In other words, do not make the Chinese look bad in any way. We just had to learn how to play the game within the game.

So it was no different as the outsider entering the inner circle of the Tianjin Gold Lions. Even though I was the coach, I was not. For the sake of face – and perhaps other reasons – I was officially known as a consultant. I ran the training sessions, but during games I had to sit behind the bench and try to have input from the second row. Fortunately, that situation changed, and I moved to the bench, but it didn't really change the in-game process.

As the game went on, I might suggest it would be a good idea to call a timeout. So, the coach – or the coach-in-title – would call a timeout. In keeping with the hierarchy, the coach-in-title would talk, the assistant coach would echo his comments, and I would have 10 seconds to offer something. The fact I had suggested the need for a timeout might have indicated I had something important to say to the team, but the coach-in-title had to be seen to be the coach. I had no problem with that, and it was not life or death. I just wanted to help the team get better.

Of course, it would have helped had I been capable of stringing together a few words of Mandarin or the players could have comprehended English better than they did. So, I had an interpreter to help bridge the language gap. During training, I would stop a drill to provide instruction or a correction. I would speak and the interpreter would speak. Only the players didn't seem very responsive. I asked the interpreter if he was passing on the message. 'Yes,' he said. 'But I have no idea what it means.' That explained part of the problem.

Even when the Chinese spoke English, I needed time to process what they were saying. While their English was better than my Mandarin, the accent did its best to sometimes confuse me. Like the time we were in Xinjiang for a game and I was told not to leave the hotel. I asked why and was told there were 'too many rubbers'. Rubbers? 'Yes, rubbers.' Ahhh. Too many robbers. Needless to say, I ignored the prospect of *rubbers* and wandered around the city in a balmy temperature of minus-14 degrees.

The Mandarin accent also provided a memorable twist for me and Margaret when she visited during the season. The locals would address us and introduce us as *Linda* and *Maggot*. While some might have objected and tried to correct them, it was easy to accept because the Chinese people, especially with the Tianjin club, were always respectful and polite. Nothing was ever too much trouble for them, which became a sore point on one occasion.

It was part of the hierarchy system that someone always carried my bags for me when we went on the road. This did not sit well with me. For two reasons: I didn't put myself above anybody, so didn't believe somebody should be designated as my personal porter; and I was not tolerant of being treated as a geriatric incompetent. Or you could just put it down to stubbornness. I protested and said I would carry my bag. The Chinese refused and I eventually gave up. Better to have tried and failed than not to have tried at all.

The communication problems did teach me one valuable lesson. Sometimes, even when instructing in a common language, we use too many words. It is better to keep it simple and as brief as possible. An explanation is not always needed to accompany the instruction. At times, I just reverted to moving a player to where he needed to be on the floor, or I offered a very poor version of Marcel Marceau, trying to mime my message.

I also kept in mind a first-hand experience of watching the coach of a Chinese junior team during a training session at Albert Park. The players were terrific athletes, but they were also typically obedient towards authority. To open training, the coach had the players stand to attention on the baseline. He then proceeded to talk at them for 20 minutes. The session that eventually followed probably squeezed out 20 minutes of productive activity. The rest of the time was taken by repetitive drills. So, I was not surprised to be walking down the streets of Tianjin just before the shops opened, and I would see the staff line-up on the footpath while the boss issued the day's instructions.

Either way, the season was a success and Tianjin gained promotion to the top division of the CBA. We were obviously a team that was good enough to play in the second division, but the competition was not elite. I didn't think anyone on the team was capable of making an Australian NBL roster, even the two Americans we had. One American was a good player to work with, smart and a good mover. The other guy was a beast but had muscles bigger than his brain. One day during training, we were running a half-court drill and I happened to look down the other end of the floor. There was our import doing chin-ups on the backboard.

My intention was to coach for one season in China, enjoy the experience and return to semi-retirement back in Melbourne, running the local Monday night comp and helping the junior Tigers teams when needed. The bosses at Tianjin had other ideas and asked me to return for the Gold Lions' first season in the CBA first division. I agreed.

There was no question the step up in divisions meant a step up in class, and the gap was quite significant when you consider some of the ex-NBA players who were and have been on CBA rosters. If Tianjin wanted to compete, and ensure a future at the top level, the club needed to bring in quality imports, better locals and persist with and develop the best young players on the youth team roster by involving them with the CBA team. That was not a message that was easily understood or accepted by the Chinese.

I was finally able to convince the club to bring three or four young players into our training sessions. It was obvious they were not immediately ready to play at that level, but with time and training, they would make rapid progress. But the hierarchy system was at work, even for those on the CBA roster. We had a young forward with a great work ethic and attitude, but he was not considered to have paid his dues. He was better than others on the team, yet he had to wait in line. The cultural system was counter-productive to winning, and so was some of the decision-making by the front office.

As we got ready for the first game of the new season, I realised our best Chinese player from the previous season was not in uniform and nowhere to be seen. I asked one of the staff about him. 'He's with another team,' the staff member replied. What?! 'We leased him to another team. We got good money for him. He will be back next year.' To say I was astonished was an understatement.

Replacing an import halfway through the season was also fraught with all kinds of problems, especially stalling tactics by the club's ultimate decision-makers. I had a connection with a prominent agent, who had placed players throughout Europe and the NBA, so I knew he could get us an upgrade on the American I wanted to replace. The Tianjin bosses agreed that we should make a change, but then the Chinese puzzle started. We had identified the replacement player, so it was a relatively simple matter of negotiating money and terms and signing the deal. But then the subtle queries started. 'Is he a better player?' 'What do we know about this player?' As much as I reassured the bosses, the more the slow-down game was played, and the deadline to make a roster change was coming fast. There was procrastination, discussion, communication and more of the same. It became clear the deal was not going to be rubber-stamped at our end, and 30 minutes before the deadline and still dealing with the agent, I was forced to admit defeat.

Learning how to deal with the people, the politics, the customs and the way of life in China is crucial for anyone hoping to work, live or study in China. Acceptance of the Chinese is important, and so is showing a willingness to bend to their ways rather than always trying to bend them towards you. Most importantly, you never show up the Chinese. In local terms, it is about saving face. We would say it is about not embarrassing a gracious host.

That even extends to the basketball court and ensuring your team does not win by too big a margin. In the opening game of the season, we won by 40 points at home. It was a good result for us. But in the return game on their court, it was a much different situation. Even though the players were exactly the same, and we were clearly a better team, we led by only six at half-time and eventually won by 12. The referees made some mind-boggling calls and they were performing a balancing act that should have been under the big-top rather than on a basketball court. The refs never allowed the result to be in jeopardy, but quite clearly knew they had to help the home team save face.

After the game, one of the referees, who I knew from international games, approached me and apologised. I understood, but he wanted to explain. 'If we don't look after the home team, nobody comes to the games,' he said. 'We have to keep it close to help promote the games.' Again, I told him I understood and there were no hard feelings. I understood the position he and his colleagues were in. But what it showed me was that Chinese basketball needs to progress beyond that mindset of saving face if it seriously wants to improve at home and internationally.

While the games during my time there were of a good standard, the refereeing was abysmal because of the need to possibly help teams stay close – or at least not get blown out. In the long run, that is a negative situation because it does not develop the players, the teams, the referees or the sport in the right way. When Chinese teams go abroad, they will not be treated so favourably by officials, who will call the game on its merits. What happens in China does not prepare players and teams for that, so it is counterproductive.

By bringing in foreign coaches to the CBA and for its national team, China appears to want to become less insulated and catch up with the rest of the basketball world. But there is always a reluctance by those running the clubs and the sport to truly give up control to foreign coaches. The foreign coach is almost always nudged into the background so a Chinese coach, who might be an inferior coach by the length of Bourke Street, is at least seen to be the man in charge. Unfortunately, until China sheds that mentality, it will struggle to make the major impact on the basketball world it so desires.

There is no question China has the population and the wealth to be a major basketball superpower. Consider that on one of the Melbourne Tigers' tours to China, we played a game against the national team that included Yao Ming, the most famous basketball player – if not sportsman – the country has produced. The game was shown on TV with a footprint through China, South Korea, Japan and the Philippines. We were told the viewership was about 300 million people. Basketball in China has the chance to expand and embrace Asia and beyond with games and leagues, but my experience in trying to organise tournaments and tours is there is always a stumbling block somewhere in the hierarchy to achieve this progress.

Even domestically, the Chinese do not seem to have a great grasp on promoting their league and games. In fact, the ability of Tianjin to promote games was highly questionable. There was basically nobody at our home games. We were playing in a city of 15 million people and you could hear when somebody dropped their popcorn during a game. There were more people playing pick-up games outside our venue than inside watching. After seeing an old guy at a few games, always sitting in the same seat and never showing a hint of emotion, I decided to approach him. He didn't know what was going on with the game. It was just somewhere to go.

All that considered, I valued and cherished my time in China with Tianjin. It was a special time in my involvement in the game and the cultural aspect was something I've treasured more than the basketball experience. Being able to observe China from within China is a rare experience for Westerners. The information and news we receive about China is not always positive. But I could easily live in China, especially in the south, where there is some unbelievably beautiful countryside.

The best thing about China is the people, who were exemplified by my interpreter at Tianjin. After finishing with the team, he drove me to the airport, and he started crying. I asked him why, and he said it was because I was leaving. He was such a genuine person and spent a lot of time trying to make a difference for himself and for others. He tried to improve basketball development within his university, and wanted to complete his Masters with research on the effects of training, physical development and recovery. That aspect of sports science and training is common in the West, but not in China, where over-training remains a big problem. Unfortunately, his tutor turned down his subject matter as being too advanced.

Undeterred, he wanted to continue studying and asked if I could recommend a university in the United States. I was able to make a connection and he received an offer. Good things happen for good people, and I only hope all good things happen to the people of China.

THE FINAL TIMEOUT

The time, date and place are not specific memories, but the feeling is one I recall all too easily. It was in the latter stages of my playing career with Melbourne Tigers and my anger was high as the team gathered in the locker room. We had just finished a game and we had been terrible, beaten by a team clearly inferior to us. We had played undisciplined, unorganised, selfish jungle-ball, which was diametrically the opposite of how I thought the game should be played. I voiced my displeasure to the rest of the team and said, 'I don't know when I will retire, but it will probably be after a game like that'.

Fortunately, I was not pushed into retirement as a player or coach by a repeat of that situation. Time and other priorities were probably the main deciding factors in both decisions to stop playing and coaching at the highest level with the Melbourne Tigers. As a player, I transitioned into a coach. As a coach, I transitioned into a fan, which was basically where I had started in the 1950s watching Ken Watson's teams play at the Melbourne Showgrounds.

After coaching the Tigers for 34 or 35 years, I had no complaints when it came time to call it quits. I had had a great run, and far better than most coaches at the elite level anywhere in the world. For a long time, I was in the unique situation of being the coach and the head of the organisation. In essence, I answered to myself so there was never any undue pressure on me to be fired or to resign. In a different circumstance, I would have been fired at some stage. Not justifiably fired, but that's just the way it goes in team sport. Just because you lose – and the Tigers lost a lot of games in their early National Basketball League years – does not mean you are not doing a good job.

I was fortunate I had the benefit of being able to remain calm when other coaches might have been stressed out. I had seen that with many coaches over the journey and I saw it with Andrew when he was coaching Sydney Kings between 2016 and 2019. The pressure of coaching the Kings might be higher than any other NBL team, but Andrew knew the deal and he handled it as he usually handled most things – with good humour. Asked via email if he was able to attend a meeting in Melbourne separate to his Kings duties, he copied me into his reply. 'I'm not in Melbourne too often given I'm coaching in Sydney until the end of the season,' he wrote. 'But if I lose the first two or three games, I might be down there very soon.' The pressure Andrew had to go through was much greater than I had to endure.

There was, of course, plenty of introspection and self-questioning over the journey. There always has to be, and if I felt there was somebody else better for the job, I would have stepped down for the sake of the club. But from 1989 to 2005, the Tigers made the NBL playoffs in 16 of 17 seasons, played in four grand finals and won two titles during what was probably the best and most competitive era of the league. Aside from the built-in pressure of winning and losing, there was also increasing pressure for the club to perform as a business. At the end of almost every season during my last 10 years in the league, the media asked if I intended to return for another season on the bench. My response was always the same. 'I always take two weeks to let the euphoria of victory or the disappointment of defeat to fully subside and then make a decision.' By the end of the 2005 NBL season, it was time to step down.

My memory is indecisive in recalling how I finally came to that decision. It was a bit like with the Australian national team. I had gone one more Olympics than intended, but I knew for sure Los Angeles in 1984 was definitely it for me. With the national team, we had something of a succession plan in place for Adrian Hurley to move up from being assistant coach to head coach, and it was the same with the Tigers. I knew the team could transition smoothly with Al Westover going from long-time assistant coach to head coach. There was absolutely no question Al deserved the chance to lead a team in the NBL, and he showed that unequivocally with four grand finals and two championships in his first four seasons.

In simple terms, I decided to retire from coaching in the NBL. With the Tigers and the NBL, that part of basketball had become a new world, a new generation and a different time. There had been difficulties recruiting, trying to keep pace with the teams who were cashed-up, and trying to balance a full-time job with coaching in a fully professional league was getting harder and harder. Andrew was also giving signals he was looking to retire from playing, so it just seemed like the right time to stand aside. That said, there were other factors that chipped away at my periphery, including the direction of the league towards another level of financial investment and corporate involvement.

As the NBL went fully professional during the 1990s, many teams got involved in something akin to a financial arms race. Teams were blatantly disregarding the salary cap, believing that if they paid for the best players, they would win a championship. By winning a title, fans and sponsors would clamour to be on board, cash would flow in and they would make money as a business. It was flawed thinking and a bad business model. After all, only one team can win the championship each year, and without a major TV deal to underpin league finances, it was more likely teams would be in the red rather than the black. The number of teams that have merged or gone under, and the number of owners who have walked away – far poorer than when they started – is testament to that. Former NBL CEO Bill Palmer once referred to team owners as astute, successful businessmen by day but pumpkin heads at night. He might have had a point with some owners.

In their early NBL days, the Tigers could hardly afford the air to pump up the basketballs. As things progressed, we were able to finance the program with some excellent and committed sponsors. The Tigers also stayed away from the quintessential private ownership model that had been adopted by almost every other team in the league, and not always with good outcomes. Unfortunately, despite the best intentions, we found ourselves in some deep financial strife. Some people forewent payments from the club, others provided loans, knowing there was a possibility that money would not be repaid. One man to step in and basically save the club as an NBL entity was Seamus McPeake, a self-made multi-millionaire in the building industry and long-time sponsor and supporter of the club. The time, money and commitment Seamus devoted to the club was enormous.

Another man, among several, who made an important contribution to the Tigers off the court was Bing Liu, who was a sponsor and became a board member. Well-educated and widely connected in China, Bing became an invaluable contributor to and promoter of the Tigers. We were always keen to find a way into China for the club, whether it be to play there, arrange tournaments and games for Chinese teams in Australia, gain sponsors or any other benefit considered appropriate. Given his connections, Bing helped us play games in China, gain a significant sponsor with whitegoods manufacturer Haier, and have our NBL games shown on Chinese TV. It is almost impossible for foreigners to do what Bing could do for us in China because he knew how to navigate the complex bureaucratic system and he had the patience and wherewithal to see the project through.

Indeed, Bing was able to provide benefits for both sides of an agreement, as he did with Haier. There was, and maybe still is, a reluctance of some Chinese to buy Chinese goods, deeming them inferior to imported goods. But if a recognisable foreigner endorsed the homemade brand, the status of the product improved. So, Bing did a deal with Haier for Andrew to endorse its brand, basically becoming an ambassador and advertising face in China. The media conference to announce the deal was attended by hundreds of TV, radio and newspaper people, which was staggering. But Andrew had become known in China, his image was good, and it became a win-win for Haier and the Tigers. It was unusual marketing, but it worked.

With the help of Seamus and Bing, the Tigers were heading in the right direction, so it seemed a good time to start thinking about moving on, firstly as coach and then from the board. After going out of the 2005 playoffs to Townsville Crocodiles, Andrew and I eventually announced our retirements as player and coach. The timing just seemed right. We had both had a good run. Better than the average player and coach and there were certainly no hard feelings or regrets the day we announced the end of the road.

In 2014, Melbourne Tigers' NBL history ended, when the franchise was renamed Melbourne United. Fortunately, Melbourne Tigers continues in its original form as a strong club with junior and senior teams, and I will be a part of that until my last day on earth.

Likewise, I thought I would probably coach at some level until my last day on earth. Not coaching at the elite level was something of a withdrawal process. I assume it is like being on drugs for three decades. It takes some time to wean off the coaching narcotic. Going to China for two seasons helped that process, and so did helping with the Tigers junior teams. But a foggy drive home from the country Victorian city of Traralgon late one Friday night – maybe it was Saturday morning – was when I knew I was cured.

I had often thought about Ken Watson's ultimate exit from coaching. The desire and will to coach never left Ken, so he would travel into Geelong from coastal Aireys Inlet to oversee a young domestic team. But age and life rapidly caught up with Ken and his family stepped in for the sake of him and others, forbidding him to drive, concerned about his cognitive capacity and even the real possibility he might fall asleep at the wheel. Only then did Ken's coaching career come to an end, not all that long before Alzheimer's disease claimed his life.

Coaching the Tigers Under-18 3 team was a role I enjoyed to a certain extent, helping the best bottom-age kids get ready to step into the 18 1s the following year. Andrew was coaching the 18 1s, so it was a good collaboration for us and the club. As the season went on, the 18 3s had developed well, were winning games and I could see a future for some of them at the next level of junior basketball. That was the positive.

The negative was one known and felt by every parent and coach who has ever been involved in junior rep basketball in Melbourne and Victoria: games scheduled for 9.50 on Friday nights around every part of the city and some parts of the state. Whoever thought that was a good idea and a way to maximise the talent in an elite junior competition needs to think again, and again, and again. Ludicrous. Driving back from eastern Victoria that Friday night, the hammer – more so than the penny – dropped. There were young coaches just as capable as me who could do the same job. While Ken Watson had to be forced to stop coaching, I got the message at 1am in the fog. I was done.

POSTSCRIPT
SPRINGFIELD

Springfield, Massachusetts is the birthplace of basketball. It was at the YMCA International Training School in 1891 that Dr James Naismith nailed a peach basket to the railing at each end of the gym and the first game of basketball took place. There were 13 original rules and the baskets were 10 feet from the floor, a measurement that has never changed. In that first game, described by Naismith as brutal, the players ran with the ball. By the second game, running with the ball had been outlawed, but the sport itself moved with such pace and popularity that it was embraced around the world and remains a global phenomenon.

Springfield, Massachusetts is also home to the Naismith Memorial Basketball Hall of Fame, and, figuratively, more than 300 people who have made important contributions to the sport. Somehow, I am among those more-than-300. According to the most recent Naismith Hall of Fame alphabetical listing, the name Lindsay Gaze is right between Dave Gavitt and George Gervin, which is just right because I was probably never as good a coach or administrator as Dave, and I was certainly never as cool or as good a player as George. All in all, I was a mixture of player, coach and administrator. Most of all, for more years than I probably care to count, I have been devoted to basketball and its people.

The honour of induction to the Naismith Hall of Fame still baffles me incredibly. I received a telephone call from Patrick Hunt, a long-time coach at the Australian Institute of Sport and one of the great contributors to Australian basketball. Always quick and ready with a joke, Pat's jovial nature can take the tension out of any situation. When he told me I was being inducted to the Hall of Fame, I chuckled and went along with him, believing it was one of his gags. Except the punch line arrived a few days later, when the official notification from Springfield arrived in North Caulfield. My immediate feeling, and throughout the whole process, was one of disbelief.

It was not the first honour bestowed on me, or the first Hall of Fame I had been enshrined in. But it is fair to say it will be the last. I have been welcomed into the halls of fame of Basketball Australia, FIBA and Sport Australia, and I am as humbled by that as I have been with every and any honour people have felt me worthy of. The reason I mention these honours is not to brag or bring them to people's attention. They are mentioned because they allow me to thank all those who helped me be recognised when so many others deserve just as many high accolades.

That was certainly an overriding feeling as I took to the stage in Springfield in 2015. With me were Larry Brown, Hank Nichols and Lute Olsen, following Hall of Fame protocol that inductees should be accompanied by enshrined veterans. The connection with all three men was long and deeply established. I had met Larry Brown at the 1964 Olympic Games, him gifting me a pair of the latest Converse shoes even though I had nothing to offer in return except for my gratitude. One of the best college referees to ever blow a whistle, Hank Nichols was an important contributor to raising the officiating standards in Australia with his visits for clinics and always being available for advice and direction, and we served together on the FIBA technical commission. Held up as one of the great college basketball coaches, Lute Olsen and his teams toured Australia, including a trip in 1996 when Arizona University played the Melbourne Tigers in the last game on Court 1 at Albert Park.

Having three familiar faces was a little comforting as I mounted the stairs to the stage for my acceptance speech in front of the world's basketball luminaries. It was daunting, and I carried a feeling of disbelief throughout the whole week. In my mind, I was an interloper and had no right to be there, but I was so grateful to meet so many people and just seeing a face often provided a memory. As I was giving my speech, I noticed Bill Walton in the middle of the audience, his face split with a grin from ear-to-ear, enjoying the whole occasion as much as anybody. I first saw Bill in 1970, when he was on the United States team at the world championship as a high school senior. While Bill only played minimal minutes in Yugoslavia, he went on to become one of basketball's greatest centres, despite suffering terrible injuries.

The whole week in Springfield was surreal, from the moment we arrived at our hotel to the time we left. There were always people asking for an autograph, people wanting to stop for a chat, people wanting a photo, people just wanting to offer congratulations. These were people I had never met in my life, but they somehow knew who I was. It was flabbergasting – in a good way – so many strangers seemed to know who Lindsay Gaze was.

For me, by far, the most important people at the Hall of Fame ceremonies and functions were my family and the people I knew. Every inductee can invite a certain number of guests and it was gratifying that people accepted the chance to attend. Among those who came to Springfield were Fred Guy, who was the Tigers' very first American import in the mid-1960s and set the standard and example – as a person and as a player – for every other American to follow; Brett Brown, who was a part of the Tigers junior and NBL coaching set-up before leading Australia at the Olympic Games, and becoming head coach of the Philadelphia 76ers; and Roger Bolton, a former Tigers junior who went from being a relatively average student at Thornbury Technical School to become the head of chemical engineering at the University of California, Davis.

Other people attended of their own volition, which was as humbling as being nominated for the Hall of Fame in the first place. Just as it was when I have received other awards and honours in settings of a much lower scale. As I recall, the Sport Australia Hall of Fame ceremony – now a lavish affair – was something like a catch-up over lunch at the St Kilda Road Travelodge.

Then there was the FIBA award ceremony I missed completely. Invited to the world championship in Turkey as recognition of being a FIBA Hall of Fame member, Margaret and I took advantage of a day off in the playing schedule to tour Istanbul. We had a terrific young guide and an excellent tour of the city. At dinner that night, a FIBA official asked me where I had been during the day. I explained about the wonderful tour of Istanbul and told him how much Margaret and I had enjoyed it. Waiting for me to finish, the FIBA official then reminded me I was to receive the Radomir Shaper Prize as recognition for service on the FIBA rules and technical committee. The presentation lunch had been that day, while Margaret and I were touring Istanbul. Apparently, FIBA had sent me an email with the details, but I never saw it. Regardless, the embarrassment on my part was acute. For the rest of the tournament FIBA assigned a minder to make sure I appeared at official functions when required.

Regardless of the size, shape or prestige of an award and the ceremony that goes with it, there are two things I always try to remember in such situations: the fame from these moments is so fleeting and quickly fades into history and out of memories; and, most importantly, they are about other people and their contributions, efforts and sacrifices just as much – maybe more in some instances – than me.

My overriding sense of pride at receiving any award is that it is a reflection on my family, Melbourne Tigers, Australia, and basketball. When I spoke at the Naismith induction, I wanted to express my gratitude to all those who have helped Australian basketball. I was simply a vehicle to get that help because of my roles in the sport, just as thousands of Australians have made excellent contributions to basketball in this country. Without those people and their extraordinary dedication as players, referees, club officials, volunteers, domestic and junior coaches, overworked staff at state associations, basketball in Australia would not be what it is today. I was fortunate to be the one recognised and I accepted my Naismith Hall of Fame induction as recognition of Australian basketball in total.

After all, I have been so fortunate to have basketball in my life for most of my life. Basketball has been my passion. It has been my vocation. It has been my sport. It helped me travel the world. It allowed me to represent my country. It took me to the Olympic Games. It provided emotional highs and lows. It opened doors of influence. It introduced me to lifelong friends and influences. It gave me a wife, who gave me a family. Quite simply, being involved in basketball from the bottom to the top for so much of my life has been a privilege and an honour.

When inducted to the Naismith Hall of Fame, I made the comment that I do not understand how I qualify for such an honour. I do not even go close to qualifying because basketball has given me so much more than I have given basketball. But I am proud to have Australia recognised and in the Hall of Fame at Springfield, Massachusetts, the true home of basketball.

LAST WORD
MAN IN THE MIRROR

I look in the mirror and who do I see?
He seems familiar, could it be me?
His eyes are watering and appear to be fading.
Some teeth are missing and the rest are shading.
Once his chest and stomach were ripped.
Now they're just soft and flabby when he is stripped.
He could jump high and take a great mark,
While playing footy in Fawkner Park.
Or other places where thousands would cheer,
As he dashed through the packs without any fear.
There was another sport and he played the game.
Olympics and basketball brought him some fame.
Along the way he took a girl on a date,
And she became his lifelong mate.
Janet and Andrew came on the scene,
And cuter babies you've never seen.
No surprise they played the game.
And also brought their own share or fame.
So life goes on to its inevitable close.
What comes after, nobody knows.
Peace for those with ended pain, hope for those who still remain.
For the man in the mirror life is rushing by.
Did he dare to do before to die?
Is there something mighty and sublime left behind to conquer time?

Lindsay Gaze

LINDSAY GAZE began his sporting career playing football with Melbourne Under 19s and Prahran in the VFA before converting to basketball. He played in three Olympic Games and coached in four. He was inducted into the Sport Australia Hall of Fame, the FIBA Hall of Fame and the Naismith Hall of Fame. He played and coached his sport as an amateur, while his professional career was as an administrator. He was General Manager of Basketball Stadiums Victoria which developed and managed the Albert Park Basketball Stadium and other stadiums in metropolitan Melbourne and regional Victoria. He was also General Manager of Basketball Victoria, taking over that position from Ken Watson in the late 1970s until he retired in 2001.

GRANTLEY BERNARD has been a sports writer since 1986 with stints at the Ballarat *Courier*, *Geelong Advertiser*, *The Australian*, and *Herald-Sun*. He has co-authored several books, including *The Andrew Gaze Story: A Kid, A Ball, A Dream*.